SCAVENGER HIKE™
ADVENTURES

and
Mountain Journal

By Kat & John LaFevre

Illustrated by G. Webb

LeConte Press

P.O. Box 222

Gatlinburg, TN 37738

LeConte Press

Scavenger Hike™ Adventures, Copyright © 2003, LeConte Press, P.O. Box 222, Gatlinburg, Tennessee, 37738   865-368-8903, scavengerhike@aol.com

Printed in the United States of America

First Printing 2003

ISBN 0-9744194-1-9

Cover painting and illustrations: G. Webb, G. Webb Gallery, Gatlinburg, TN.

Cover and graphic design: Rainbow Graphics, Kingsport, Tennessee

Printed at Quebecor World, Kingsport, Tennessee

Caution: Outdoor hiking, by its nature, is potentially hazardous. All hikers must assume responsibility for their own actions and safety. All of the hikes are on designated portions of the Great Smoky Mountains National Park trails. It is impossible to list or describe all potential hazards. National Park brochures and publications by the Great Smoky Mountains Association provide additional safety information. The park is a wild area and should be treated with utmost safety and common sense. Nature may change or alter some of the Scavenger Hike treasures. The trail search hints will be constantly reviewed and regularly updated.

What *Is* a Scavenger Hike Adventure . . . Anyway???

The mountains are calling! Grab your family or friend! **A wilderness adventure is waiting for you!**

Scavenger Hike Adventures are challenging and fun for amateur hikers, experienced day hikers, and serious trekkers!!! Hikes range from an easy half-mile to a challenging ten miles and <u>over</u> a mile high in elevation!!!

Five scavenger hikes are kind of <u>Easy,</u> five are <u>Moderate</u> and four are <u>Extreme</u>! All 14 hikes lead to exciting discoveries!!!

Are *you* up for the challenge? Follow our clues and find . . . a tree clawed open by a bear searching for food . . . an ancient Indian footpath . . . a wrecked steam engine that rolled off a mountain over 80 years ago . . . hidden breath-taking mountain views . . . a beautiful waterfall view that almost all visitors never get to see . . . remains of an old Model T deep in the forest . . . pioneer cabins . . . and <u>over 200 other unusual treasures</u>!

Earn 10 points **for each treasure that you find and achieve** *one of three certificate levels!!!* **Finally answer the question!!!**
Are you a ......???
<u>**City Slicker!**</u>
<u>**Pioneer Scout!!**</u>
<u>**or Frontier Explorer!!!**</u>

We have included <u>**Scavenger Hike Adventures**</u> near campgrounds and <u>throughout</u> the national park! **Don't *Just* Take a Hike . . . Take a Scavenger Hike Adventure!!!**

SCAVENGER HIKE ADVENTURES

"Don't *Just* Take a Hike . . . Take a Scavenger Hike Adventure!!!"

Contents

What *Is* a Scavenger Hike Adventure . . . Anyway???   iii
The Great Smoky Mountains National Park, A Treasure   ix
Beyond Description!
Who Are Your Scavenger Hike Adventure Guides?   x
Our Thanks   xi
What's All This Talk About Bears???   xii
Top Ten Day Hiker Checklist   xiii
Mountain Journal   138
Keep Exploring The Smokies! Here Are Some Great Books!!!   152
Order Form   154

#1   "Junglebrook" Noah "Bud" Ogle Farm Trail   Page 1

- 3/4-mile loop, about an hour, the trail is rocky, shaded, pretty easy

#2   Porter's Creek Trail to Old Hiking Club Cabin   Page 11

- 2 miles roundtrip, 2–3 hours, trail has long gentle uphill slope, wide, not very hard, moderate

#3   **Laurel Falls Trail to Laurel Falls**   Page 22
(stroller accessible and wheelchair do-able)

• 2.6 miles roundtrip, about 2 hours, trail is paved, gentle uphill
slope, popular, pretty easy but not a cakewalk

#4   **Appalachian Trail (AT) (EXTREME)**   Page 31
to Charlie's Bunion (a pinnacle rock overlook)

• 8 miles roundtrip, allow 5 hours, trail is rough,
steep, worth the effort (EXTREME)

#5   **Trillium Gap Trail to Grotto Falls**   Page 42

• 3 miles roundtrip, about 2 hours, trail has a few
uphill slopes, wide, popular, a little harder than
Laurel Falls, moderate

#6   **Big Creek Trail to Midnight Hole**   Page 52
and Mouse Creek Falls

• 4 miles roundtrip, 2–3 hours, definitely not crowded,
level, wide trail, moderate

#7   **Sugarlands Valley Nature Trail**   Page 63
(wheelchair/stroller accessible)

• 1/2-mile loop, less than an hour, trail is paved, level, short, easy

#8 **Cades Cove to Abrams Falls Trail** Page 74
to Abrams Falls
• 5 miles roundtrip, 3–4 hours, wide trail
has some solid uphill slopes, popular family
hike, moderate

#9 **Fighting Creek Nature Trail** Page 86
• 1-mile loop, 1 hour or less, trail climbs a bit
uphill here and there, still quite easy

#10 **Smokemont Nature Trail** Page 96
• 3/4-mile loop, less than an hour, trail is narrow,
up-over-around and down a mountain, easy

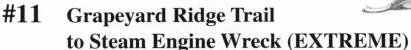

#11 **Grapeyard Ridge Trail** Page 103
to Steam Engine Wreck (EXTREME)
• 6 miles roundtrip, allow 3–4 hours, trail has
a long ridge climb, many unbridged shallow
streams, fairly secluded (EXTREME)

#12 **Cosby Nature Trail** Page 113
• 1-mile loop, about an hour or less, pretty
level, shaded, easy

#13/14 Alum Cave Bluffs Trail to the Bluffs
(MODERATELY EXTREME) and Up to
Mount LeConte (EXTREMELY EXTREME)

To Alum Cave Bluffs and back (#13)

- 4.4 miles roundtrip, 3–4 hours, level at first, some long climbs, kind of tough in spots (MODERATELY EXTREME)

Continuing on from the bluffs to Mt. LeConte (#14)

- About 10.5 miles roundtrip (includes hiking on top of Mt. LeConte)

- 6–8 hours, even your high school gym teacher would be challenged by this trail!!! (EXTREMELY EXTREME)

The Great Smoky Mountains National Park
A Treasure Beyond Description!

There simply are no words or photographs that
can capture the *majesty, warmth,* and *beauty*
of the mountains or the *friendly sound* of
a little red boomer squirrel chattering in
the early morning mist.

There is only one way to *feel the magic*
of a waterfall or *sense the awe* as
a deer quietly walks through the forest.

You must experience it!!!

Please remember that you are entering *a
very fragile and diverse system* of plants,
water, and animals that is *known and
cherished throughout the world.*
There are over 1,500 unique flowering plants,
over 130 different species of trees, and
scientists believe there are over 100,000
different life forms.

Please protect our national treasure . . .
The Great Smoky Mountains National Park!

Please . . .
Take Only Pictures
Leave Only Footprints.

WHO ARE YOUR SCAVENGER HIKE ADVENTURE GUIDES?

Kat and John LaFevre are Gatlinburg, Tennessee, locals who live in a log cabin high up in the mountains. They are avid hikers and love the Great Smoky Mountains. They have hiked and researched the trails and visited with many old-timers to discover the hidden natural and historical treasures of the Smokies.

Kat has a bachelor and master's degree in Elementary Education, taught for several years, and now works as a VIP (volunteer in the Great Smoky Mountains National Park). She is also assisting with the national park's Outreach Program, an educational community initiative. Kat is working on her goal to hike all of the nearly 850 miles of trails in the park.

John majored in English and Communications and is a business consultant and motivational speaker. He has written feature articles for the *Wall Street Journal*'s National Employment Weekly and many national magazines. He has also written a business book which was published by Simon & Schuster and issued in three editions. John is a country musician and songwriter when he is not out on the trails or talkin' somewhere.

Our Thanks

Our thanks to the park rangers, volunteers, and professional employees of the Great Smoky Mountains National Park for the outreach programs, ranger led hikes, and special park events that were invaluable resources as we researched hidden treasures.

In particular, thanks to George Minnigh, Backcountry Specialist with the national park system, Ellen Ogle, Resource Education Ranger, and Marion Kloster, Forestry Technician. They reviewed our drafts and offered invaluable insight and encouragement. We are fortunate to have them working for all of us in our national park.

Thanks to Annette Hartigan, Park Librarian, Mike Jenkins, Ecologist, and Don Jones, Park Volunteer, for assisting us in validating facts and species.

Thanks to Ken Jenkins, nationally acclaimed wildlife photographer who founded "Wilderness Wildlife Week," an event that brings together wilderness and wildlife experts every year to share stories and knowledge. What a wonderful learning experience.

Thanks to the Great Smoky Mountains Association and Friends of the Smokies who sponsor many educational programs. These two non-profit organizations exist for the sole purpose of protecting and enhancing the park for all visitors and future generations.

We also thank esteemed artist and friend, G. Webb, for painting the cover and illustrating our book.

A special thanks to Lori LaFevre, University of Tennessee student, Joel Outten, graduate student at UT, and Mark Bryant, student at Pittman Center School for field testing the trails. Thanks to Amy and Kevin VanDeWater for proofreading, editing, and encouragement. Finally, our thanks again to the Great Smoky Mountains Association for their wonderful library of publications, which were an invaluable resource.

WHAT'S ALL THIS TALK ABOUT BEARS???

Want to see a bear? Keep in mind that most bear sightings occur in the early mornings and at dusk. Our favorite way to go "lookin' for bears" is to rent *bicycles* at the Cades Cove campground area. Try to be the first customers on those mornings when the park *does not* allow cars into Cades Cove and bike around the 11-mile loop, just you, your bike, and wildlife!!! Of course, Cades Cove is also a great place to search for wildlife from your car! Don't miss it!!!

- **There are about 2,000 or so black bears living in the park. That means there are about two bears for every square mile.**

- **You'll find bears out and about in the early morning or at dusk, but also throughout the day and night. There could be one around the next bend in the trail. Bears do not want to harm you. They just want to be left alone so they can go about their "bear" business.**

- **If you see a bear, remain watchful and *DO NOT APPROACH IT!!!***

- **NEVER RUN FROM A BLACK BEAR!!! Slowly back away.**

- **If a bear is persistent in following you, then talk loudly, shout at it, clap your hands, raise your arms to look bigger, and even throw non-food objects at it if necessary. (See park visitor centers for additional info.)**

- **If a black bear attacks you . . . fight back!!! Never play dead or lay down.**

- **Bears can run and climb up and down trees much faster than you!!!**

Final note that "bears" consideration: **Don't feed the bears!!!** Once a bear tastes peanut butter or fried chicken and potato salad, they want seconds and thirds. Then they see "people" as a food source and they often lose their natural fear of humans and become what is called a "nuisance" bear. These bears often must be removed from the park and sometimes even killed because they threaten people by getting too close. Remember . . . people food kills bears!!!

SCAVENGER HIKE ADVENTURES

<u>TOP TEN DAY HIKER CHECKLIST</u>

1. Always protect the Great Smoky Mountains National Park! Treat it like the "treasure" that it is! Don't pick anything! Don't take anything! Don't leave anything!

2. Stay on the trails! Step lightly! Respect and protect each and every plant and animal in the park!

3. Don't forget to pack your common sense. This is a wilderness area!

4. Water is the most important item for you to bring! Never drink from streams and rivers!

5. Bring snacks or lunch along! Food tastes at least twice as good in the woods!

6. Always plan on some raindrops falling on your head! Bring a poncho! If the weather forecast calls for 100% sunshine . . . bring your poncho!

7. Insect repellent is a handy item especially in the summer!

8. Hiking boots are great! Gym shoes are "fine." Sandals . . . not recommended. Wear flip-flops and that is just what you will do! *When counting steps to find treasures . . . small folks take tall steps and tall folks take small steps!*

9. Wet rocks and roots can be very slippery! Please watch your step!

10. Most hikers who have gotten lost separated and went ahead of their group! Stay with your exploration party and have a great Scavenger Hike Adventure!

GREAT SMOKY MOUNTAINS

Scavenger Hike Adventure #1

<u>"Junglebrook"</u>
<u>Noah "Bud" Ogle Farm Trail</u>

<u>**Why This is a Great Trail!**</u> This Scavenger Hike Adventure is *awesome!* You will find a pioneer cabin and barn that is about 120 years old and a *working* water-powered grinding mill deep in the forest! The pioneers called this area "Junglebrook" because the woods are overgrown like a jungle! You'll cross many log footbridges over small streams. You'll even cross some streams with *no bridges!* You'll search for an old-fashioned water pipe, umbrellas over your head, a "drive-thru" pioneer barn, a hidden hillside spring, a place where a bear might be napping, and much more!!!

<u>**Where's the Trail?**</u> From the Sugarlands Visitor Center go north on Rt. 441 into Gatlinburg. Turn right (east) at <u>**Stoplight #8,**</u> Historic Nature Trail/Airport Road (Stoplights in Gatlinburg are all numbered with big signs). Follow the signs to Roaring Fork Motor Nature Trail and the Ogle Place. Parking is on the right.

About the Trail: This Scavenger Hike Adventure is on a beautiful easy trail which crosses streams and runs along LeConte Creek. There are rocks along the trail ranging in size from beachballs to beanbag chairs and much larger! It is pretty much all level with a couple of small hills to climb. "Junglebrook" is mostly shaded in the thick woods making this a *very cool* trail! If this trail wasn't free—we would *guarantee* double your money back if you don't think this Scavenger Hike Adventure is awesome!!!

How Long Is This Hike? This Scavenger Hike Adventure is a 3/4-mile loop and will take about an hour to complete.

Things to Hunt For
(Earn 10 points for each treasure you find)

#1 FIND THE QUARTZ ROCK SMACK-DAB BETWEEN TWO TREES!!! NEAR START OF TRAIL BEFORE MARKER #1

SPECIAL HINT: You'll find this reddish-brown and white quartz rock smack-dab between two trees! After you find it look around! Most of the trees that you see here today were *not here* when this was a pioneer farm. In fact, all around you were open fields and a big apple orchard!!! As you head up to the cabin, you'll be walking on the old road that led to Gatlinburg (back then Gatlinburg was called White Oak Flats). Farmers needed their land for food so the roads often ran beside or at times even *in* the creek so land would not be wasted. The Ogle family planted and raised all their own food!!!

_____**10 points**

2

#2 FIND GRANNY'S WINDOW!!! IN THE OLD LOG CABIN

SPECIAL HINT: Find the small window with a wooden "door." It was called "granny's window!" Granny Ogle could sit by the window and open it for fresh air or shoot at foxes that were after her chickens (according to a former resident). Women had to protect the family's food from wild animals especially when the men were away. Can you believe there were four beds in this one room! This early pioneer cabin is about 120 years old!!!

_____**10 points**

#3 FIND THE LOFTS WHERE THE BOYS WOULD SLEEP!!! LOOK UP

SPECIAL HINT: Look up and find where the Ogle boys would sleep! Sorry! No girls were allowed to sleep up there in the loft! Bud and Cindy Ogle and their four boys and four girls lived in this cabin! At first, the cabin only had one room, but they needed more space for all the young'uns so they built another room on the other side of the fireplace! Check it out! Cindy called the original room of the cabin "the house" and the room they added on she called "t'uther"!!!

_____**10 points**

#4 FIND THE RHODODENDRON JUNGLE!!! HEAD INTO THE WOODS PAST MARKER #3—STEP ON THE ROCKS TO CROSS THE STREAM

SPECIAL HINT: Look all around you! Rhododendron have long, narrow, leathery, evergreen leaves. They are so thick here that the pioneers called this area "Junglebrook!" Imagine in the summer when the rhododendron flowers were all in bloom! Mountains! Green forest! Flowering bushes! White rushing waters! "Junglebrook" was a beautiful and peaceful place! It still is!!!

_____**10 points**

#5 FIND THE HUGE STUMPS OF OLD CHESTNUT TREES!!!
GO 40 STEPS PAST THE LOG FOOTBRIDGE

SPECIAL HINT: Start lookin'! All the huge chestnut trees died over 70 years ago from a bad blight (disease). It was said that cabins made from chestnut trees would last forever because the wood would never rot. The chestnuts were *delicious* and bears were much bigger back then because they ate lots and lots of chestnuts! Hogs loved them, squirrels loved them, wild turkeys loved them, and people loved them too! Ahhh . . . Chestnuts roasting o'er an open fire!!!

_____10 points

#6 FIND A TREE THAT LOOKS LIKE TWINS!!!
ON THE RIGHT SIDE OF THE TRAIL—BETWEEN
MARKER #5 AND MARKER #6

SPECIAL HINT: Find the two trunks of a tree that are joined together at the bottom. Then . . . from this tree, walk <u>42</u> steps toward marker #6 and search for another twin tree on the right! I guess you could say you found "twin twin twees"!!! The twunks of these twees were split by nature when they were very young. The twees may have been stwuck by lightning or chewed on by an animal to make them split and grow "twin twunks"!!!

_____10 points.

#7 FIND AN OLD ROCK WALL BUILT BY THE PIONEERS!!!
ON BOTH SIDES OF THE TRAIL

SPECIAL HINT: The Smoky Mountains is a very rocky place. Rock walls were built by pioneers to clear the rocks *off* the land so crops could be planted, cabins could be built, and cows could be kept out of the garden and in the pasture. The pioneer children helped build these walls! The area all around you was once a large cow pasture. After you find the wall, *mooooove* along!!!

_____10 points

#8 FIND WHERE THE HONEYMOON CABIN ONCE STOOD!!!
ABOUT 30 STEPS PAST THE ROCK WALL—ON THE LEFT OF THE TRAIL

SPECIAL HINT: A huge stack of rocks marks the spot of the "honeymoon" or "weaner" cabin. Bud and Cindy Ogle would let their sons and their new brides live here for one year until they could build a cabin of their own. When the Ogle *girls* married, they moved on with their husbands.

_____10 points

#9 FIND AN OLD-FASHIONED WATER PIPE!!! SEARCH ACROSS THE PATH FROM THE HONEYMOON CABIN

SPECIAL HINT: Find a long log that was *carved out* to carry water. *Please stay on the trail.* You'll see such log flumes *in use* in about five minutes. The Ogles didn't have metal pipes, but these carved-out logs worked just great to bring water from LeConte Creek to the mill!!!

_____10 points

#10 FIND "UMBRELLAS" OVER YOUR HEAD!!! AFTER YOU PASS THE CARVED-OUT HOLLOW LOG—WATCH FOR THE *NATURE TRAIL* SIGN BY THE PATH—STOP AT THE SIGN AND TURN RIGHT

SPECIAL HINT: Follow the side path all the way down to LeConte Creek! *Small children should be escorted down to the stream. Remember . . . rocks may be slippery!* When you get to the stream *look straight up* to find the *"umbrellas"* over your head!!! These leaves are from the umbrella magnolia tree. The Smoky Mountains gets more rain than almost anywhere else in our whole country. In fact, about seven feet of rain or more falls in the upper elevations every year. Umbrellas sure come in handy in the Smokies!!! These "umbrellas" are not available in the winter or early spring when the leaves are gone.

_____10 points

#11 FIND THE OLD PIONEER FAMILY TUB MILL!!! ON THE RIGHT OF THE TRAIL

SPECIAL HINT: Walk inside and then go up the wooden steps and then peek down through the hole and see the waterwheel that turns the corn-grinding machine. This <u>tub mill</u> would grind corn into cornmeal and then the Ogles could make cornbread! There used to be about 13 tub mills on this creek! That's why back then they called this stream "Mill Creek." The mill was a popular place for the mountain folks to get together and *"spin yarns," "tell tall tales,"* and catch up on news of the *locals* while the *young'uns* played in the creek. People were always *"milling around"* the mill!!!

_____10 points

#12 STOP AND PLOP DOWN ON A ROCK!!!
JUST PAST THE TUB MILL

SPECIAL HINT: Sit on a rock and listen to the water to get these points! See the water . . . hear the water . . . and then follow the hollowed out logs upstream to the log dam and see where they *catch* the water!!! ***Be careful on the slippery rocks!***

_____10 points

#13 FIND WHERE A BEAR MIGHT BE TAKING A NAP!!!
HEAD *WAY* UP THE HILL—TO THE *VERY TOP*—LOOK ON THE LEFT OF THE NATURE TRAIL SIGN

SPECIAL HINT: Look for a big flat rock that is *almost,* but not quite, level with the ground, like a platform that completely fills the area between the two trees. Stand on the rock, look away from the path and find the <u>dark holes in the rocks</u> on the side of the hill. Do you think a bear could be taking a nap in there? Remember! Now that "Junglebrook" is part of our national park, many of the "locals" that live here today make their homes among the rocks and in the trees!!!

_____10 points

#14 FIND TARZAN'S GRAPEVINE!!! WALK UP THE TRAIL AND THEN TAKE 20 STEPS <u>BACK</u> FROM MARKER #9 TOWARD MARKER # 8— LOOK TO THE LEFT

SPECIAL HINT: Look deep into the woods on the left and find a humongous woody wild grapevine high up in the trees! You might just be tempted to give a Tarzan yell! On second thought . . . let's not disturb the "locals"!!!

_____10 points

#15 FIND THE BOULDER THAT IS BIGGER THAN YOUR CAR OR TRUCK!!! ON THE RIGHT OF THE TRAIL

SPECIAL HINT: You don't need a special hint for this one! You'll know when you find *this* giant boulder!!! Can you find the thin strand of white quartz rock that runs through this boulder? Veer to the right after you pass the boulder and stay on the rocky trail.

_____10 points

7

#16 FIND THE TREE THAT A GIANT WOODPECKER PUNCHED HOLES IN BIG ENOUGH TO STICK YOUR HAND INSIDE THE TREE!!! 25 STEPS UP THE TRAIL FROM THE CORNER OF THE BIG BOULDER YOU JUST FOUND— LOOK ON THE LEFT

SPECIAL HINT: A pileated woodpecker is a giant black and red crested bird that pecks giant oval holes in trees. It is the largest and loudest woodpecker in all of North America!!! It looks like the famous cartoon character, Woody Woodpecker. "That's all folks!!!"

_____10 points

#17 FIND A PERSON IN YOUR GROUP WHO HAS SOME FOOD OR A SNACK!!! EXPLORE AROUND BACKPACKS OR BULGING POCKETS

SPECIAL HINT: *Say,* **"Doh-YUST zah-ah-geest?"**

That is Cherokee for *"What have you got to eat?"* Cherokee Indians lived all around these mountains long before the white settlers came. Cherokees still live in these mountains on the Qualla Indian Reservation in Cherokee, North Carolina. Chief Sequoya saw white settlers holding paper with writing on it and he called it "talking leaves." He wanted Cherokees to have "talking leaves" so he made a symbol for every Cherokee sound and Cherokees began to learn their new written language! So . . . keep reading this "talking leaf" and head on down the trail!!!

_____10 points

#18 FIND THE FALLEN TREE THAT LANDED ON A BIG ROCK!!! NEAR MARKER #10

SPECIAL HINT: This tree would have fallen all the way to the ground but on the way down a boulder caught it instead. Very nice catch!!!

_____10 points

#19 FIND A WALL OF ROOTS!!! HIKE FOR ABOUT 5 MINUTES—CROSS STREAMS SEVERAL TIMES—LOOK ON THE LEFT OF THE TRAIL

SPECIAL HINT: Look for two trees that fell over and created an incredible <u>wall of roots</u>. Nature is amazing!!!

_____**10 points**

#20 FIND A "DRIVE-THRU" BARN!!! NEAR MARKER #12

SPECIAL HINT: Walk thru—the Drive-thru!!! This "<u>drive-thru barn</u>" is over 120 years old! Can you believe Bud Ogle built this barn almost all by himself!!! Bud and his sons could load hay on a wagon and then drive right through the barn to unload the hay and feed the animals!!! There were a few other buildings on this old farmstead, including a smokehouse, a springhouse, a hog pen, and a corn crib. Travelers on the wagon road in front of the barn would stop by to feed and water their animals. They were charged a "toll" (small fee) by the Ogles for this service.

_____**10 points**

#21 FIND THE HIDDEN MOUNTAIN SPRING!!! PAST THE BARN—ON THE SIDE OF THE HILL

SPECIAL HINT: This hole is where the Ogle family got their water from a spring. Remember the hollowed out logs you saw at the tub mill? The Ogles used the same kind of logs to bring water from this spring all the way to the back porch of their cabin where all the *washin'* was done. Most folks had to carry their water in big heavy buckets and that was hard work! The Ogles were one of the first families in the area to have automatic "running water"!!! Their neighbors thought this was pretty cool!!!

_____**10 points**

CONGRATULATIONS!!!

YOU HAVE JUST COMPLETED A
GREAT SMOKY MOUNTAINS NATIONAL PARK

SCAVENGER HIKE ADVENTURE!!!

"Junglebrook"
Noah "Bud" Ogle Farm Trail

TEN POINTS FOR EACH ITEM FOUND

TOTAL SCORE _____

CERTIFIED ACHIEVEMENT

LEVEL_____

over 50 to 100 points: **City Slicker**
over 100 to 180 points: **Pioneer Scout**
over 180 points: **Frontier Explorer**

Name(s): _____

_____

Witness(es) thereof: _____

Date: _____

GREAT SMOKY MOUNTAINS

Scavenger Hike Adventure #2

Porter's Creek Trail
to Old Hiking Club Cabin

Why This Is a Great Trail! This Scavenger Hike Adventure winds along the beautiful Porter's Creek rapids in the *quieter and less busy* Greenbrier section of the national park. This trail is *loaded* with historic artifacts from the old pioneer days! Find the special "mountain rock" where the pioneers "courted" (went on dates) and the remains of a Model T hidden deep in the forest! You will search for a special tree that the Indians used, cross log footbridges, and stand in an old "refrigerator" (spring house) that is *still* cooled by running water! You will find an old cabin with bunk beds built right into the walls, an old outhouse, and much more! We'll give you some good hints, but you can't be dozin' on this hike. Pick yourself up by the bootstraps! Let's go!!!

Where's the Trail? From the Sugarlands Visitor Center go north on Rt. 441 into Gatlinburg. Veer right at **Stoplight #3,** just past the Hard Rock Café (Stoplights in Gatlinburg are all numbered with big signs). Follow US 321 approximately 6 miles to the Greenbrier entrance of the Great Smoky Mountains National Park. Turn right. Travel the narrow road along the incredibly beautiful whitewater of the Little Pigeon River and follow the signs to Porter's Creek trailhead. You'll pass the ranger station and go deep into the woods past the picnic area. There's a parking area at the trailhead. You will never regret the *beautiful drive* to get to this Scavenger Hike Adventure!!! There will be *at least* five "Ooohs" and "Ahhhs" along the way!!!

About the Trail: This Scavenger Hike Adventure is a gentle *uphill* hike on a trail wide enough for an automobile. That means you can look forward to a gentle *downhill* slope all the way back.

How Long Is This Hike? This Scavenger Hike Adventure is 2 miles roundtrip and will take 2–3 hours to complete.

Things to Hunt For
(Earn 10 points for each treasure you find)

#1 FIND THE OLD CORNFIELD THAT NO LONGER *LOOKS* LIKE A CORNFIELD!!! CROSS THE VEHICLE GATE TO START THE TRAIL—LOOK TO THE RIGHT OF THE TRAIL

SPECIAL HINT: Search for a group of over 50 trees with grayish bark, that are straight, very tall, thin, and look like *giant pencils!* These are yellow poplar trees (tulip trees) that often grow up in what was once a cornfield. Some folks think the leaves or the spring blossoms on this tree are shaped like tulips. To get the points, "erase" those pencil-shaped trees from your mind and visualize the cornfield! Greenbrier was once a bustling farming community with over 800 people living here! Isn't that amazing?

_____10 points

#2 FIND THE TWIN YELLOW BIRCH TREE THAT THE INDIANS USED!!! AS YOU HIKE UP THE GENTLE SLOPE LOOK TO THE RIGHT—IT IS ONLY 2 FEET (24 INCHES) OFF THE TRAIL

SPECIAL HINT: This yellow birch tree has split into two trunks and you might think it looks like a "twin" tree. It has yellowish/silverish (sometimes shiny) bark that, in places, looks like shredded paper! The grooves/lines in the bark run *horizontal* to the ground instead of *vertical.* That is a major clue! What is cool about this unusual tree is that there is oil in the bark, so pioneers and Indians could use it to start fires *even when the bark was wet!* We get lots of rain in the Smoky Mountains so this tree was probably *very much* appreciated!

_____10 points

#3 FIND THE "DEVIL'S WALKING STICK"!!! ON THE RIGHT SIDE OF THE TRAIL—ONLY 2 FEET OFF THE TRAIL

SPECIAL HINT: As you walk up the hill, *first— find the cliff in an open area* overlooking the creek—*way down there!* On the opposite side of the trail from this cliff area, find a tree about the thickness of a hiking stick. It is covered with hundreds of thorns! Pioneers called it the "Devil's Walking Stick." It looks like a hiking stick with thorns! Ouch!!!

_____10 points

#4 FIND THE "MOUNTAIN ROCK" WHERE YOUNG PIONEERS WENT ON DATES!!! ON THE LEFT SIDE OF THE TRAIL

SPECIAL HINT: This giant rock *does* have a shape like a mountain and your eyes would have to be closed to miss this natural wonder! Young pioneers would meet here to "court" (date). Obviously, this was a long time before funnel cakes, miniature golf, and the sky lift in Gatlinburg were invented!!!

_____10 points

#5 FIND THE GIANT TURTLE ROCK!!! ABOUT 175 STEPS PAST THE MOUNTAIN ROCK—STOP AND LOOK AHEAD ABOUT 30 YARDS ON THE RIGHT SIDE OF THE TRAIL—FIND THE "TURTLE" STICKING HIS HEAD OUT OF A SHELL

SPECIAL HINT: This may sound like Ripley's Believe It Or Not, but the pioneer young'uns who got bored dating at the "mountain rock" would also date at the "turtle rock"! It really *does* look like a turtle sticking his head out of his shell!!!

_____**10 points**

#6 FIND A SALAMANDER!!!
STOP AT THE LITTLE MOUNTAIN STREAM THAT CROSSES THE PATH

SPECIAL HINT: Carefully lift up stones or small branches that are in or along the water. Underneath these rocks and sticks are the homes of salamanders. In the Smokies, salamanders grow from 1/2-inch to over 2 feet long!!! *Be gentle, don't ever put a rock back on top of a salamander or keep it out of water for more than a minute because its skin will dry out*. There are more salamanders in this national park than the total of birds, deer, bears, and all other mammals combined!!!

_____**10 points**

#7 FIND THE GIANT *OLD* OAK TREE THAT IS SEARCHING FOR WATER!!! NEXT TO THE MOUNTAIN STREAM ON THE RIGHT SIDE OF THE TRAIL

SPECIAL HINT: The roots are growing all around rocks to search for water! In the Smokies you'll see lots of tree roots growing on top of the ground because they have trouble getting through the rocks. The Smoky Mountains is a very rocky place! There are many very *old* trees in the park. The Great Smoky Mountains National Park also has more *champion* trees (largest of the species) than any other national park in the United States!!!

_____**10 points**

#8 FIND AND SIT ON THE LOG BENCH!!!
ON THE LEFT

SPECIAL HINT: This hike is a gradual uphill climb and this is a mandatory break point. You deserve the break and the points for making it this far!

_____10 points

#9 FIND AN AWESOME CASCADE!!! 35 STEPS PAST THE BENCH

SPECIAL HINT: A cascade happens when water flows over and around rocks. If the water level here is normal, you will see a breathtaking cascade in the creek at this point. It is a great spot to have a snack and definitely a place to pause and relax for a minute!

_____10 points

#10 FIND A DYNAMITE HOLE THAT WAS DRILLED IN A ROCK!!! A COUPLE OF FEET TO THE RIGHT OF THE CENTER OF THE TRAIL

SPECIAL HINT: Look down! Keep searching as you walk up the trail! In the 1930s, during the Great Depression, President Franklin D. Roosevelt started the Civilian Conservation Corps (CCC). Over 4,000 unemployed young men from all over the United States were hired to help build many of the trails, roads, and stone bridges in this park. They were paid $30 per month and were required by CCC rules to send most of the money back home. These young men lived in camps throughout the park. They sometimes used dynamite to blast rocks out of the way.

_____10 points

#11 FIND THE HALF-MILE-LONG ROCK WALL!!!
LOOK DEEP INTO THE WOODS ON THE RIGHT

SPECIAL HINT: Keep looking to the right, up on the ridge, to find the wall. Pioneers had to clear the rocks off their land so they could plant crops and build cabins. "VanderBill" Whaley was a wealthy settler who got his nickname from the wealthy Vanderbilt family. He was not related to them. He lived here in Greenbrier with his wife and ten children. His daughters did a lot of the rock work around their house. Rock walls also helped keep animals out of garden areas and often followed along property lines.

_____**10 points**

#12 FIND THE 13 ROCK STEPS THAT LEAD UP TO "VANDERBILL'S" HOME SITE!!! ON THE RIGHT SIDE OF THE TRAIL

SPECIAL HINT: *Be careful* as you walk up the rock steps to pay a visit to this old pioneer's homesite! *It is always wise to look before you step just to be sure you do not step on a Smoky Mountain critter (possibly a snake). Also watch where you reach with your hands just to be on the safe side!* VanderBill's daughters were very proud of the wall and the steps they helped build leading to their cabin. How did the girls move all of those heavy rocks, anyway? The rocks were put on sleds and then pulled to the wall!!!

_____**10 points**

#13 FIND "VANDERBILL'S" FIREPLACE!!! FOLLOW THE PATH
THROUGH THE BUSHES AT THE TOP OF THE ROCK STEPS

SPECIAL HINT: Find the fireplace and imagine where this big four-room home was located. Remember VanderBill was wealthy! He also owned a mill! If you had your *own* mill, you could grind your *own* corn and also charge others a "toll" to grind their corn. Having a mill could provide extra income for a family.

_____**10 points**

#14 FIND THE CELLAR WHERE THE WHALEYS KEPT POTATOES!!! "WARM" YOUR <u>BACK</u> AT THE FIREPLACE (WHERE THE FIRE WOULD HAVE BEEN)—THEN LOOK OUT AND DOWN AT THE GROUND

SPECIAL HINT: Look for a low spot or depression in the ground. This area was the cellar. It was a *cool* place to store things that needed to *stay cool*. How *cool* is that? Head back down the 13 steps to the trail.

_____**10 points**

#15 FIND A "HEADACHE CURE" AT THE BRIDGE!!!
LOOK TO THE RIGHT AS YOU STAND ON THE BRIDGE

SPECIAL HINT: Find an evergreen plant. Think . . . very long leaves and very long name—<u>rhododendron</u>! You'll find rhododendron throughout the Smokies. They bloom in the late spring and summer. These shrubs in front of you are *rosebay* rhododendron and have beautiful white or light pink blooms. *Catawba* rhododendron grow in the upper elevations and have beautiful big purple and pink blooms! Pioneers made tool handles out of the wood. Cherokee Indians carved pipes and toys out of this shrub and believed a leaf on the forehead would cure a headache! Please use your own aspirin or headache cure! *Don't ever pick or harm any plant in the park. All plants are protected by our national park laws.*

_____**10 points**

#16 FIND THE REMAINS OF AN ANTIQUE MODEL T!!! FIND
THE CEMETERY STEPS ON THE RIGHT SIDE OF THE TRAIL—COUNT <u>115
STEPS</u> FROM THE CEMETERY STEPS CONTINUING ON THE TRAIL—
LOOK TO THE RIGHT AND PEER INTO THE WOODS ABOUT 30 YARDS OR
SO

SPECIAL HINT: Look for rusted fenders and parts! Notice how wide the
trail is? Why do you think it is so wide? Hint: Don't you wish you had a Model T
right now? By the way, those cemetery steps that you passed lead to a cemetery with
headstones marked Whaley, Ownby, and Proffitt. They were some of the earliest settlers and their names are *still* popular throughout the county.

_____**10 points**

*NOW, JUST ENJOY THE HIKE! WHEN YOU COME TO THE SPLIT
OR "Y" IN THE TRAIL BEAR TO THE RIGHT. WHEN YOU COME
TO A SMALL SIGN THAT SAYS **"Historic Farm Site,"** HEAD 200
YARDS TO THE RIGHT.*

#17 FIND THE TAX-SAVING BARN!!! DON'T WORRY ABOUT
FINDING IT—THIS BARN WILL FIND <u>YOU</u>!!!

SPECIAL HINT: The second level of the barn extends farther out than the
lower level. It is called a <u>cantilever</u> barn. It is a copy of a German design. In Ger-
many you only had to pay *taxes* for the amount of actual *ground* your barn was sitting on. You didn't have to pay taxes for the larger overhanging part of the second
level. Pioneer John Messer built this barn in 1875, over 125 years ago!

_____**10 points**

#18 FIND AND THEN STAND INSIDE AN OLD "REFRIGERATOR"!!! GO STRAIGHT THROUGH THE BARN— FOLLOW THE SHORT PATH TO THE SPRING HOUSE

SPECIAL HINT: Water from the spring would flow right through the spring house and keep potatoes, eggs, milk, and other foods cooled. Go ahead, stand inside the "pioneer refrigerator"!!!

_____10 points

#19 FIND THE BOXWOOD BUSHES!!! ON THE RIGHT AS YOU FACE THE FRONT OF THE CABIN

SPECIAL HINT: These bushes are not native to the park. They were planted to decorate around the cabin. There are small dark-green leaves on the round-shaped boxwoods.

_____10 points

#20 FIND THREE ROUND MILLSTONES!!! IN THE AREA IN FRONT OF THE CABIN

SPECIAL HINT: They look like bicycle-sized round wheels except they are made out of stone. They are half-buried in the yard. The round stones would spin around and against each other in a tub mill and crunch down the corn into cornmeal. Don't you wish you had some cornbread and beans right now?

_____**10 points**

#21 FIND THE BUNKBEDS!!! ATTACHED TO THE WALLS OF THE CABIN

SPECIAL HINT: Go inside and explore throughout this cabin! Years ago the cabin was used by a hiking club. Check out the amazing inside lock on the back-door of the cabin. It looks like it was designed to keep out big black bears! Can you figure out how the lock works?

_____**10 points**

#22 FIND THE OUTHOUSE!!! OUT BACK OF THE CABIN

SPECIAL HINT: Follow the path out back, out yonder! You do not have to go inside or even get close to the outhouse to get the points!!!

_____**10 points**

CONGRATULATIONS!!!

YOU HAVE JUST COMPLETED A
GREAT SMOKY MOUNTAINS NATIONAL PARK

SCAVENGER HIKE ADVENTURE!!!

Porter's Creek Trail
to Old Hiking Club Cabin

TEN POINTS FOR EACH ITEM FOUND

TOTAL SCORE _____

CERTIFIED ACHIEVEMENT

LEVEL_____

over 50 to 100 points:	**City Slicker**
over 100 to 180 points:	**Pioneer Scout**
over 180 points:	**Frontier Explorer**

Name(s): _____

_____

Witness(es) thereof: _____

Date: _____

GREAT SMOKY MOUNTAINS

Scavenger Hike Adventure #3

<u>Laurel Falls Trail to Laurel Falls</u>

<u>Why This Is a Great Trail!</u> This Scavenger Hike Adventure is on a beautiful mountain trail that you *don't want to miss!* It leads to Laurel Falls, which has an incredible 85-foot drop along a beautiful rock face! What a great spot to relax and have some trail mix! You will find an awesome view of this double waterfall that most visitors will never get to see! You will search for a stream that *never* runs dry, a favorite snack of Smoky Mountain northern flying squirrels, jammed up rocks, and mountain views that are simply breathtaking! You will find some great "Kodak" or "digital" moments on this trail!!!

<u>Where's the Trail?</u> From the Sugarlands Visitor Center (an awesome "<u>must see</u>" place to visit!) the trail is 3.8 miles southwest on Little River Road. There is <u>no sign</u> for Little River Road so just follow the signs toward Cades Cove, Townsend, and Elkmont. If you enter the parking lot at Sugarlands Visitor Center, turn right as you leave the parking lot to get on Little River Road. The falls and the parking area for the trail are well marked.

About the Trail: This trail was so popular that it was paved in the 1960s to prevent erosion and is now _easily accessible for strollers and "do-able" for wheelchairs._ You will find benches and rocks along the way to take a break or two! It is a gradual ascent of only 300 feet in a mile, but the benches still come in handy for most folks! _Rocks are slippery around the falls._ **Be careful!!!** _There are some sheer drops as you get closer to the falls._ **Watch the kids!!!**
Actually, there is an upper and lower falls!
Two waterfalls for only one hike! Gotta be one of the best deals around town—even beats those free samples of fudge!!!

How Long Is This Hike? This Scavenger Hike Adventure is about 1.3 miles to the falls (2.6 miles roundtrip) and will take most pioneers less than 2 hours.

Things to Hunt For
(Earn 10 points for each treasure you find)

#1 FIND MOUNTAIN LAUREL AND RHODODENDRON!!!
NEAR MARKER #1

    SPECIAL HINT: Look all around! You are standing right in front of rhododendron and mountain laurel bushes, two of the _most popular shrubs_ in the entire park! To get the points, find out which is which! Here's how to tell the difference between the two. Long leaves equal long name (rhododendron) and shorter leaves equal shorter name (laurel). They both have dark-green, thick, leathery leaves. Their flowers bloom all along this trail in the spring (mountain laurel) and summer (rhododendron) and the leaves stay green year-round! Pioneers actually called rhododendron "laurel" and called mountain laurel "ivy." Now you know why this is called _Laurel_ Falls Trail!!!

_____**10 points**

#2 FIND THE JUNGLE!!!
45 STEPS FROM MARKER #1

SPECIAL HINT: "No lions, no tigers, just bears, Oh my!!!" The rhododendron grows so thick here that it feels like a jungle! The rhododendron was so hard to walk through that pioneers called it a "laurel hell." Peer into the woods and find the tangled shrubs. The rhododendron leaves are also "thermometers!" When the leaves darken and droop it is about 32 degrees! At around 20 degrees the leaves roll up and then at 0 degrees the leaves roll up as tight as a pencil! How cool is that? A free outdoor thermometer!!!

_____**10 points**

#3 FIND A PINE TREE THAT WAS KILLED BY SOUTHERN PINE BEETLES!!! 12 STEPS PAST MARKER #2
ON THE LEFT

SPECIAL HINT: This pine tree was *killed by an insect* known as the southern pine beetle. Woodpeckers probably went after the beetle larvae and pecked little holes in the tree to find them. Dead trees become "home" for many forest critters including salamanders, small mammals, and insects!

_____**10 points**

#4 FIND THE SECOND GROWTH FOREST!!! AT MARKER #3
LOOK DOWN IN THE HOLLER

SPECIAL HINT: Find lots of smaller trees! This area was logged and also had a huge forest fire. That is why the trees in the "holler" are smaller than a lot of the older trees that live farther up the trail past the waterfall. The loggers didn't go that high up the mountain to cut down trees. In fact 3/4 of a mile past Laurel Falls are some of the oldest trees in the park! You can find trees up there that are hundreds of years old!!!

_____**10 points**

#5 FIND THE UNUSUAL TREE TWISTED BY THE WIND!!!
50 STEPS FROM MARKER #3—ON THE RIGHT—LOOK UP

SPECIAL HINT: The high winds can cause branches to curve in strange directions! We mean _really_ strange directions!!!

_____**10 points**

#6 FIND A TREE GROWING RIGHT THROUGH AN 8-FOOT-HIGH BOULDER!!! BETWEEN MARKER #3 AND MARKER #4

SPECIAL HINT: You really don't need a hint on this one. Just look to the right and find the tree that broke through a boulder as it grew. This tree was so determined to grow through this rock we should probably name it "Rocky"!

_____**10 points**

#7 FIND THE BENCH BY THE STREAM THAT NEVER RUNS DRY!!! JUST PAST MARKER #5

SPECIAL HINT: Take a break! Of the more than 2,000 miles of streams in the Great Smoky Mountains, this one never runs dry! Deer, bears, snakes, otters, coyotes, and salamanders are a few of the animals that drink from this stream. Many plants and trees thrive along the mountain streams. ***Never drink from a mountain stream*** unless you treat the water with chemicals or boil it! Microscopic critters live in the water and can make you very sick! Hey! Find the octopus behind the bench!

_____**10 points**

#8 FIND ROOTS CLIMBING ON AND OVER A LARGE GROUP OF ROCKS!!! AFTER A SHARP LEFT TURN AT A GROUP OF JAGGED ROCKS—HIKE UP THE HILL—LOOK ON THE RIGHT

SPECIAL HINT: There's not much soil up here due to erosion but there are lots of rocks in the Smokies! The trees have to send out roots searching for soil and water. Can you match up a root with its tree? The roots go over, under, around, and through rocks to get something to eat and drink!!! As one tree said to another, "Where is a Food City when you need it?"

_____**10 points**

#9 FIND THE SMOKY MOUNTAIN "PRODUCE DEPARTMENT"!!! ACROSS THE TRAIL FROM MARKER #6—LOOK TO THE LEFT IN THE WOODS FOR BLUEBERRY BUSHES

SPECIAL HINT: Squirrels, chipmunks, birds, and, of course, bears, love this area because of all of the produce— nuts (acorns), berries, and seeds. To a bear, this area is "blueberry heaven" or maybe even "bearadise"! If you sit on the log bench, you'll see a blueberry patch on the left and the right.

_____**10 points**

26

#10 FIND BLANKET MOUNTAIN!!! AT MARKER #7—LOOK FOR THE HIGHEST MOUNTAIN PEAK IN THE DISTANCE

SPECIAL HINT: In 1802 surveyors were establishing the boundary line for a treaty with the Cherokee Indians. A brightly colored blanket was hung on a tree on top of this mountain to help mark the spot. Ever since then, that highest peak has been called Blanket Mountain. This is definitely a "Kodak" or "digital" moment! If you feel the urge you might want to say, **"Ooosh sgwah nickt!!!"** Cherokee for, "That's incredible!!!" Cherokee Indians lived around the Smoky Mountains long before white settlers arrived. They called the Smoky Mountains **"Shaconage"** (pronounced Shuh-kon-a-gee), which means "land of blue smoke."

_____**10 points**

#11 FIND THE GROUP OF JAMMED UP ROCKS!!! ABOUT 46 STEPS PAST MARKER #8—LOOK ON THE RIGHT

SPECIAL HINT: These rocks were pushed up from pressure deep inside the earth. They were kind of "squished" out of the earth. Some scientists believe the continents slowly collided millions of years ago causing this tremendous pressure. It is believed the Smoky Mountains are over 260 million years old and many of the rocks here are over 600 million years old!!! Whoa!!!

_____**10 points**

#12 FIND THE ROCK TRIPE!!! NEAR MARKER #9

SPECIAL HINT: Look up high on the boulders to your right. This rock tripe looks like _brownish (sometimes greenish) crumpled leaves_. It is a scaly lichen (pronounced "like-in"), which is a combination of algae and fungus, and it grows right on the rock. The rock tripe has acid in it and it gradually eats away at the rock. The very tiny particles of broken rock eventually become soil. _Rock tripe is a favorite snack of northern flying squirrels!_ Look! Up in the sky! Is it a bird? Is it a plane? No, it's a northern flying squirrel!!! Actually, they are nocturnal so you'll usually only see them at night and they generally fly around in higher elevations.

_____**10 points**

#13 FIND THE DYNAMITE HOLE!!! GO 5 STEPS PAST MARKER #9—SEARCH ON THE RIGHT

SPECIAL HINT: Workers had to dynamite and blast through the mountain when they built this trail years ago. Look around for a round hole drilled in the rock to hold a stick of dynamite!

_____**10 points**

#14 FIND BRIGHT YELLOW LICHEN!!! PAST MARKER #9 ON THE RIGHT SIDE OF THE TRAIL—ON THE ROCKS

SPECIAL HINT: This lichen (still pronounced "like-in") looks like <u>bright yellow spray paint</u> on the rocks. Lichen comes in many different colors. There are over 600 kinds of lichen in this national park! This is a bright one!

_____**10 points**

#15 FIND THE DRIPPING ROCKS !!! ON THE RIGHT

SPECIAL HINT: You'll know you have found them when you see a big rock you can sit on *right* in front of the dripping rocks.

_____**10 points**

#16 FIND GALAX—THE SHINY LEAF USED BY FLORISTS!!!
ABOVE THE DRIPPING ROCKS

SPECIAL HINT: Look for the green *shiny* leaves growing right above the dripping rock ledge. The leaves are shaped kind of like fat hearts and the plants are quite short and low to the ground. The leaves turn crimson red in the fall. Mountain folks earned money gathering the galax leaves for florists. *Remember never pick anything . . . these plants are protected by national park laws. Those who break the laws could be given a very sizable fine.*

#17 FIND LAUREL FALLS!!! FOLLOW YOUR EARS

SPECIAL HINT: Laurel Branch tumbles down from Cove Mountain about 46 feet before it lands in the pool! Then the pool spills over a ledge and drops another 39 feet! Whoa!!! It rains a lot in the Smoky Mountains (over 7 feet each year in the higher elevations), which helps make the beautiful waterfalls!!!

_____**10 points**

#18 FIND THE VIEW OF THE UPPER AND LOWER FALLS!!!
50 STEPS PAST THE BENCH AT THE FALLS

SPECIAL HINT: *Walk very carefully* up the unpaved rocky, rooty trail past the falls for another 50 steps. Turn around and you will see the entire upper and lower parts of the falls! Most visitors never see this view. Awesome!!!

_____**10 points**

CONGRATULATIONS!!!

YOU HAVE JUST COMPLETED A
GREAT SMOKY MOUNTAINS NATIONAL PARK

SCAVENGER HIKE ADVENTURE!!!

<u>Laurel Falls Trail</u>
<u>to Laurel Falls</u>

TEN POINTS FOR EACH ITEM
FOUND
TOTAL SCORE _____

CERTIFIED ACHIEVEMENT
LEVEL_____

over 50 to 100 points:	<u>**City Slicker**</u>
over 100 to 160 points:	<u>**Pioneer Scout**</u>
over 160 points:	<u>**Frontier Explorer**</u>

Name(s): _____

_____

Witness(es) thereof: _____

Date: _____

GREAT SMOKY MOUNTAINS

Scavenger Hike Adventure #4

Appalachian Trail (AT) to Charlie's Bunion (EXTREME)

Why This Is a Great Trail! This Extreme Scavenger Hike Adventure takes place on the world famous *Appalachian Trail!* This is the "Real McCoy," the "Big Kahuna," one of the longest continuous trails on planet earth!!! (2,143 miles long from Georgia to Maine.) The AT runs along a ridge and you will find breathtaking views of North Carolina mountains on one side and postcard views of Tennessee mountains on the other! You will find Mt. LeConte's landslide, Icewater Spring backcountry campsite, a breathtaking 1,000-foot sheer cliff drop, and a view of the highest point in all of the Smokies *from* some of the highest points! People from all around the world have hiked the AT! **Now it's your turn!!!**

Where's the Trail? From Sugarlands Visitor Center travel on Rt. 441 toward Cherokee, North Carolina, to Newfound Gap (13 winding mountain miles with incredible scenic pull-offs all along the way). Park at Newfound Gap and you'll see the trailhead sign for the AT as you head up the ridge.

About the Trail: This part of the AT is very rocky, sometimes steep and narrow, sometimes muddy, and runs along a high elevation ridge leading to Charlie's Bunion, a bare rock pinnacle overlooking many majestic valleys below. We recommend that you start the hike mid-morning to <u>allow time for the clouds to clear off the trail!</u> ***Caution: There are exposed cliffs as you get closer to the peak!***

How Long Is This Hike? This hike is 8 miles roundtrip and will take *about* 5 hours. We suggest you take a lunch and a nap at Charlie's Bunion!!!

<u>Things to Hunt For</u>
(Earn 10 points for each treasure you find)

#1 FIND THE NORTH CAROLINA/TENNESSEE STATE BOUNDARY LINE!!! LOCATED AT NEWFOUND GAP

SPECIAL HINT: Up until the 1850s there was another "gap" or route over the Smokies called "Indian Gap." Then guess what? Someone discovered this better *"new found gap."* Some describe this location as the centerpoint of the Smokies. About half of the Great Smoky Mountains National Park is in Tennessee and the other half is in North Carolina. When was the last time you had the opportunity to straddle two states?

_____10 points

#2 STAND IN THE SHOES OF PRESIDENT FRANKLIN D. ROOSEVELT!!! USE THE DISPLAY BOARD AS A GUIDE

SPECIAL HINT: Stand in the exact spot where FDR dedicated the Great Smoky Mountains National Park in a ceremony on September 2, 1940. Thousands of people once lived in what is now the national park. The people of Tennessee and North Carolina raised about half the money ($5 million dollars) to buy the land from private owners and businesses so it could become a park. Even the schoolchildren saved their pennies to help. Then John D. Rockefeller, a wealthy businessman, took care of the other half.

_____10 points

#3 FIND OUT HOW MANY STATES THE APPALACHIAN TRAIL (AT) RUNS THROUGH!!! LOOK NEAR THE TRAILHEAD

SPECIAL HINT: You are about to hike on one of the most famous trails in the world! About 70 miles of the AT runs through this national park. Most of the trail is deep in the wilderness and not easily accessible. *Make sure your shoestrings are tied!!!*

_____10 points

#4 FIND THE WHITE BLAZE!!! AS YOU HEAD UP THE TRAIL LOOK ON THE TREES TO THE RIGHT

SPECIAL HINT: Whether in Maine or Georgia or in-between, the painted white rectangle is the symbol that you are not lost—you are on the AT!!! For 2,143 miles you will be guided by the "white blaze." Today, the blaze will guide you all the way to Charlie's Bunion!!!

_____10 points

#5 FIND THE DEAD FOREST OF FRASER FIR TREES!!! LOOK ON BOTH SIDES OF THE TRAIL AT THE FIRST 90-DEGREE LEFT TURN

SPECIAL HINT: The balsam wooly adelgid ("a-dell-jid") insect came to the United States from Europe about 100 years ago and showed up in the Smokies in 1963. These tiny insects killed thousands of mature fraser fir trees throughout the park! You will walk directly under a dead fraser fir tree up ahead. Such a powerful tree brought down by such tiny insects! Tens of thousands of insects infested and sucked the sap and the life out of each tree.

_____10 points

#6 FIND THE COMBINATION ROCK RAIN COVER AND REST BREAK AREA!!! AFTER YOU CLIMB A ROCKY HILL SEARCH ON THE RIGHT

SPECIAL HINT: This small cave-like opening is a perfect spot to duck out of the rain or just take a load off! Hey! Any sign you're still on the AT?

_____10 points

#7 FIND THE NEWFOUND GAP ROAD!!! 100 STEPS PAST THE CAVE-LIKE OPENING AS THE TRAIL LEVELS A BIT— LOOK TOWARD NORTH CAROLINA (TO YOUR RIGHT)

SPECIAL HINT: The road is located *out and down!* This road twists and turns its way from Gatlinburg, Tennessee, to Cherokee, North Carolina. Unless you want to drive about a "billion" miles, it is the only way to get between these two cities. This is the only road in the park that cuts across the mountains.

_____10 points

PUT YOUR BOOK AWAY UNTIL YOU REACH THE 1.7-MILE INTERSECTION WITH SWEAT HEIFER CREEK TRAIL. SETTLERS WOULD BRING THEIR COWS UP THIS TRAIL TO GRAZE. YOU KNOW IT IS STEEP WITH A NAME LIKE "SWEAT HEIFER."

#8 FIND THE HIDDEN POSTCARD VIEW OF NORTH CAROLINA!!! LOCATED ON SWEAT HEIFER CREEK TRAIL—GO 70 STEPS FROM THE SIGN FOR THE TRAIL

SPECIAL HINT: Get off the AT at this intersection (mile 1.7) and go right on Sweat Heifer Creek Trail heading toward Kephart Shelter. Go 70 paces from the sign at the intersection with the AT and you will find a rough opening for a private rest break with a view that will *knock your hiking socks off!* After your break, <u>DON'T FORGET TO GET BACK ON THE AT!!!</u> Turn **right** onto the AT.

_____**10 points**

#9 FIND THE LONG AND WINDING ROAD!!! AS YOU HEAD UP A STEEP GRADE—TAKE THE SHORT 8-FOOT-LONG SIDE PATH TO THE RIGHT OF THE AT

SPECIAL HINT: Look for the Newfound Gap Road switching back and forth around a huge mountain. You can see the entire switchback from this spot!!! The Cherokee word **"Shaconage"** (pronounced Shuh-kon-a gee) means "the land of blue smoke." The blue haze is caused by "zillions" of plants and trees releasing vapor into the air.

_____**10 points**

#10 FIND CLINGMAN'S DOME RAMP AND OBSERVATION TOWER!!! LOCATED ACROSS (SOUTH AND RIGHT) FROM THE ROCKY CLEARING NEAR THE TOP OF THE RIDGE

SPECIAL HINT: This is an incredible view of layers upon layers of mountain ridges! Clingman's Dome is the highest peak in the park at 6,643 feet! Look southwest to the highest mountain range in the distance and on a clear day you can see the outline of the tower. If you don't have a compass, just look out yonder to your far right. Binoculars or someone related to an eagle would be a good thing to have on hand at this juncture!

_____**10 points**

#11 FIND THE SPRUCE FIR FOREST!!! HIKE A WHILE—THEN SEARCH ON BOTH SIDES OF THE TRAIL AS YOU FINALLY BEGIN TO HEAD DOWN THE SLOPE—THANK GOODNESS FOR DOWNHILL!!!

SPECIAL HINT: You are walking through a forest of red spruce and fraser fir trees. Red spruce have very short needles that are pointed and sharp. The needles are about an inch long. A fraser fir tree's needles are longer, flat, and are whitish on the underside. You could conduct a scientific test by touching the ends of the needles. If it hurts, it is probably a red spruce. If it doesn't hurt at all, it is probably a fraser fir. Thank goodness for science!!!

_____**10 points**

SPECIAL NOTE: Between the spruce fir forest and Icewater Spring is a log on the left of the trail that was *hot-iron branded* with the AT symbol! Pretty cool if you find it!!!

#12 FIND THE "MILLION FEET GULLEY"!!! HIKE A WHILE—BEAR RIGHT TOWARD CHARLIE'S BUNION AT THE INTERSECTION WITH THE BOULEVARD TRAIL (AT MILE 2.7)—THE BOULEVARD TRAIL LEADS TO MOUNT LECONTE (NOT TODAY, FOLKS!!!)

SPECIAL HINT: Hike downhill for a few minutes and notice the deep gully. This gully was created by millions of hikers *like you* trodding down on the mud and dirt. It keeps getting deeper and deeper!!!

_____**10 points**

#13 FIND ICEWATER SPRING BACKCOUNTRY SHELTER!!!
ABOUT A QUARTER MILE PAST THE INTERSECTION WITH THE
BOULEVARD TRAIL

SPECIAL HINT: Look for the narrow path to the right. It will lead to the shelter. Find the shelter's fireplace and unique "privy" (a restroom facility in the middle of the wilderness). There are about a dozen backcountry shelters in the park for use by backpackers. A lot of folks who stay in this shelter are hiking on the AT all the way from Maine to Georgia or from Georgia to Maine! They are called "thru-hikers." There is a guest book for comments by those who sleep in the shelter. Take a look! Very interesting!!!

_____**10 points**

#14 FIND THE BEAR AVOIDANCE FOOD PULLEY AND HOIST SYSTEM!!! LOCATED NEAR THE ICEWATER SPRING SHELTER

SPECIAL HINT: Look for a wire and pulley system between two trees that hikers use to hoist up their backpacks and food so bears cannot get to them. Bears are also attracted to toothpaste, hairspray, and shaving cream! ***You don't want nothin' that smells in that shelter!!!*** There are about 2,000 black bears walking around in this park. It's been said that a bear can climb up a tree faster than you can fall out of a tree!!!

_____**10 points**

#15 FIND SIGNS OF WILD HOGS!!! EXPLORE AROUND THE ICEWATER SPRING SHELTER AND FURTHER UP THE APPALACHIAN TRAIL

SPECIAL HINT: Look for areas on the ground that wild hogs rooted up with their snouts to find acorns and plants to eat. Wild hogs *also* eat snakes, snails, small mammals, salamanders, and bird eggs and can weigh up to 300 pounds. Some park rangers are employed *full-time* to hunt for hogs because they *are not* native to the park and they destroy plants, pollute the streams, and eat animals that *are* native to the park. In the 1940s someone had a bad idea to bring some wild boars from Europe to a game preserve in North Carolina. They got loose, bred with farmers' pigs in the Smokies, and about 10,000 of them have been removed from the park since then. Hundreds still roam the park at night!!!

_____10 points

#16 FIND THE ICEWATER SPRING!!! AS YOU LEAVE THE
SHELTER AND GO RIGHT ONTO THE AT— LOOK FOR
A METAL PIPE IN A SMALL STREAM OF WATER CROSSING
THE TRAIL

SPECIAL HINT: This is a very high elevation spring and the
water is really cold. Some say it is as cold as _____ _____!!!

_____**10 points**

*PUT YOUR BOOK AWAY FOR THE
FINAL MILE TO CHARLIE'S BUNION.*

#17 FIND CHARLIE'S BUNION!!! THE APPALACHIAN
TRAIL HAS A BUNION BYPASS TO THE RIGHT AS YOU
APPROACH THE BUNION—<u>BEAR TO THE LEFT</u> WHEN YOU
REACH THAT SPLIT IN THE TRAIL—YOU'RE ONLY 100 YARDS
FROM THE BUNION!!! YES!!!

SPECIAL HINT: A fire in 1925 burned off all the vegetation on Charlie's
Bunion and four years later a heavy rain washed off all of the roots on this rocky
pinnacle. Horace Kephart, a writer and park supporter, asked George Masa, a photographer and <u>Charlie Conner</u>, a local mountaineer, to help him survey the damage.
Charlie's foot was hurting by the time they reached the rock vista and later when
Kephart sat on a special committee to name places in the park, he suggested to name
this pinnacle "Charlie's Bunion." Charlie Conner later said that he <u>never really had a
bunion.</u> We applaud Kephart because we think "Charlie's Bunion" is a much better
name than "Charlie's Achin' Foot!!!"

_____**10 points**

#18 FIND MT. LECONTE!!! LOOK NORTHWEST (LEFT) OF CHARLIE'S ACHIN' FOOT—I MEAN CHARLIE'S BUNION

SPECIAL HINT: Look across the valley from Charlie's Bunion, an incredible sheer drop with a very scenic pinnacle. Look for the mountain that has great scars (stripped area brownish in color) to find Mount LeConte, the third highest peak in the park. A flash flood on Labor Day weekend in 1951 tore off vegetation on the north slope of Mount LeConte. The only resort lodging in the park is on top of that mountain! The food is brought to the lodge on the backs of llamas! Wouldn't it be nice if llamas showed up *right now* with fried chicken, potato salad, ice cold sweet tea, and pineapple upside-down cake? Oh well . . . pass the trail mix please.

_____**10 points**

#19 FIND MASA KNOB!!! LOOK FOR THE ROCK PEAK RIGHT BEFORE YOU REACHED CHARLIE'S BUNION

SPECIAL HINT: Remember the name of the photographer in Kephart's group in item #16? Just think. If Kephart would have asked *you* to come along to survey the damage, this pinnacle might have been named after *you! How's your feet?*

_____**10 points**

CONGRATULATIONS!!!

YOU HAVE JUST COMPLETED A
GREAT SMOKY MOUNTAINS NATIONAL PARK

SCAVENGER HIKE ADVENTURE!!!

Appalachian Trail (AT) to
Charlie's Bunion (EXTREME)

TEN POINTS FOR EACH ITEM
FOUND

TOTAL SCORE _____

CERTIFIED ACHIEVEMENT
LEVEL_____

over 50 to 100 points: **City Slicker**
over 100 to 130 points: **Pioneer Scout**
over 130 points: **Frontier Explorer**

Name(s): _____

_____

Witness(es) thereof: _____

Date: _____

GREAT SMOKY MOUNTAINS

Scavenger Hike Adventure #5

<u>Trillium Gap Trail</u> <u>to Grotto Falls</u>

<u>**Why This Is a Great Trail!**</u> This Scavenger Hike Adventure is on a beautiful trail with giant trees that are hundreds of years old! The trail leads to an incredible water-fall with a 25-foot drop. You will find a crystal clear pool of water at the bottom of the falls. You can walk *right behind* Grotto Falls!!! You will search for salamanders in some great places to find them! Keep your eyes wide open because this is the only trail in the park where you just might see a <u>llama</u>! Llamas use this trail to carry sup-plies up to the rustic lodge at the top of Mt. LeConte. You will be hiking along one of the steepest streams in the park (Roaring Fork) with water tumbling all the way down from Mt. LeConte over a half-mile above you! You'll find a few streams that you must cross with no footbridges! Happy rock hopping!!!

<u>**Where's the Trail?**</u> From the Sugarlands Visitor Center go north on Rt. 441 into Gatlinburg. Turn right (east) at <u>**Stoplight #8**</u>, Historic Nature Trail/Airport Road (stoplights are all numbered in Gatlinburg). Follow the signs to the <u>Roaring Fork Motor Nature Trail</u>. The Trillium Gap trailhead, which leads to Grotto Falls, is at Marker #5 on the motor trail. It is well marked by a sign.

About the Trail: This is a moderately sloped wide dirt trail. Grotto Falls is a *well-hiked* and *well-liked* trail! An extra bonus on this Scavenger Hike Adventure is that to get to the trailhead you must travel on the <u>Roaring Fork Motor Nature Trail!</u> This is a one-way narrow 5-mile loop through dense forests passing many beautiful streams and restored cabins. It can best be described as a "mountain hike" for your car! Your car will absolutely love it!!! This road is closed in the winter months.

How Long Is This Hike? This Scavenger Hike Adventure is about 3 miles roundtrip. You should allow a couple of hours for this hike.

Special Comment: If you continue on past Grotto Falls for another 1.7 miles you will reach a beautiful "heath bald" on top of <u>Brushy Mountain</u>. A "heath bald" is an area covered with shrubs from the heath family such as catawba rhododendron, mountain laurel, and sand myrtle. Trees seldom grow there because of the thin soil and harsh environment at the higher elevations. Narrow paths cut through the heath bald and lead to some of the most awesome views you'll ever see! You will feel like you are standing on top of the world! It is pretty steep to get there so if you are huffin' and puffin' at the falls you may want to go on back down the hill. If you ain't huffin'—don't miss the pinnacle views from the top of Brushy Mountain!!! The views will take your breath away if the hike up hasn't already!

Things to Hunt For
(Earn 10 points for each treasure you find)

#1 FIND A PAVED CORN FIELD!!! AS YOU PARK YOUR VEHICLE

SPECIAL HINT: This parking lot was once an open field of corn! In fact, the road you traveled on to get here, Roaring Fork Motor Nature Trail, was once a rough wagon trail leading to Gatlinburg. The Roaring Fork community was settled about 160 years ago. In the early 1900s about two dozen families made Roaring Fork their home. My how times do change!!!

_____**10 points**

**#2 FIND A *BIG* . . . NO, I MEAN *HUGE* . . . NO, I *REALLY*
MEAN . . . *GARGANTUAN* HEMLOCK TREE!!!** HEAD UP THE
TRAIL—LOOK ON THE RIGHT SIDE OF THE TRAIL—SO CLOSE YOU
COULD TOUCH IT WITH A HIKING STICK

> **SPECIAL HINT:** Look for dark-reddish-brown bark on a *huge* tree with branches of needles that some folks think look lacy! To know for sure that you found the correct tree, look for a boulder at the base of the tree with a little skinny stripe of white quartz rock running through it. You are standing in an old growth forest! That means that this part of the forest wasn't logged or farmed. Some of the humongous trees along this trail are hundreds of years old! Some of the trees in old growth forests in the Smokies are over 500 years old!!!

_____**10 points**

**#3 FIND THE TREE GROWING ON A FLAT PLATE OF
ROCK!!!** GO 17 STEPS FROM THAT *GARGANTUAN* TREE YOU JUST
FOUND—SEARCH ON THE RIGHT

> **SPECIAL HINT:** Trees somehow just manage to deal with all the millions of rocks in the Smoky Mountains! Tree roots sometimes break right through rocks to search for food and water!!! You'll see more examples up ahead on the right. These trees let nothing stop them. They just "Rock On!!!"

_____**10 points**

#4 FIND A LLAMA TRAIL!!! GO UP THE HILL—FIND THE SIGN
FOR <u>TRILLIUM GAP TRAIL</u>—HEAD TOWARD GROTTO FALLS

SPECIAL HINT: Trillium Gap Trail leads llamas and people to a rustic resort over a half-mile above you at the top of Mt. LeConte. You can make a reservation and hike up there and spend the night. Llamas will bring you a great dinner and breakfast! They carry the food and clean sheets and pillowcases on their backs! Llama hooves are padded and smaller than horses' hooves and cause much less damage to the trail. Keep your eyes wide open. You just might see a llama!!!

_____**10 points**

#5 FIND THE WILD AND CRAZY BROWN WOODY
GRAPEVINES!!! CROSS THE STREAM—COUNT 65 STEPS PAST THE
STREAM—SEARCH ON THE LEFT

SPECIAL HINT: Look up at the wild and crazy woody grapevines climbing this way and that way all over the trees! Opossums, skunks, bears, and other critters in the Smokies enjoy eating the sour wild grapes. Long ago, Cherokee Indians who lived in this area believed that burning grapevine wood and oak together would bring a spell of warm weather in the middle of a cold winter!

_____**10 points**

#6 FIND A "ZILLION" FERNS!!! AFTER A SHARP RIGHT TURN IN THE TRAIL—WALK ABOUT 1 MINUTE AND LOOK ON THE MOUNTAINSIDE

SPECIAL HINT: These <u>ladyferns</u> have very dainty leaves that are delicate and look like green lace. This fern is beautiful and there are "zillions" of them all along this trail. Many different types of ferns grow in both moist and dry environments in the Smoky Mountains.

_____10 points

#7 FIND A SIGN OF A BEAR!!! LOOK ALL ALONG THE TRAIL— <u>BUT BE CAREFUL THAT YOU DON'T MISS #8</u>

SPECIAL HINT: Look for signs of bears all along the trail! Search for logs or lower portions of trees that have been clawed, ripped apart, or shredded by bears looking for termites, grubs, and other insects to eat. There are many examples along the trail. There are about two black bears for every square mile in this park (about 2,000 bears in total). <u>Go on to #8 as you keep your eyes wide open for signs of bears!</u>

_____10 points

#8 FIND A TALL TREE STUMP THAT USED TO BEND OVER THE HOLLER WITH HUNDREDS OF SHOOTS GROWING UP FROM THE BASE!!! IT WILL TAKE A LITTLE WHILE TO GET TO THIS TREE—LOOK ON THE LEFT AS THE TRAIL HEADS UPHILL AND BENDS TO THE RIGHT

SPECIAL HINT: <u>Hundreds of little shoots</u> are growing at the base of the trunk. This is a <u>basswood tree</u>! It has heart-shaped leaves. The tall tree used to bend over the holler and you can find the rest of the tree on the ground. Bees swarm the yellow flowers of basswood when they bloom in early summer. Basswood honey was a favorite of mountain folks. Cherokee Indians and others used the basswood for carving. Pioneers would hollow out basswood logs to make barrels.

_____10 points

#9 FIND A BEAR MATTRESS!!! STAND AT THE EDGE OF THE SMALL STREAM THAT CROSSES THE TRAIL—LOOK ON THE RIGHT AND BACK BEHIND YOU

SPECIAL HINT: These shrubs are found all throughout the park. Their long, thick, and narrow leaves are evergreen. Rhododendron have beautiful flowers in late spring and early summer! Bears sometimes gather the branches of leaves to use for bedding in winter dens. *Remember, don't take anything or pick anything or leave anything! In other words, protect this awesome place!!!*

_____**10 points**

#10 FIND A PARTRIDGE BERRY NOT IN A PEAR TREE!!! LOCATED ON THE HILLSIDE NEAR THE RIGHT SIDE OF THE TRAIL

SPECIAL HINT: This partridge berry plant grows low to the ground and has tiny dark green leaves with a very noticeable white vein in the middle of each leaf. To get the points, you must find a red berry or a white blossom! Look all along the mountainside as you continue toward the falls. *Be "berry" careful to protect the berries and every plant in this park. Please leave them for all to see!*

_____**10 points**

#11 FIND THE "BIG BIRD" BEAK!!! HIKE AWHILE—CROSS ANOTHER STREAM—THEN PASS A HUGE HEMLOCK TREE IN THE MIDDLE OF THE TRAIL WITH BIG ROOTS AND <u>CLEAR PATHS GOING AROUND THE TREE ON THE LEFT AND THE RIGHT</u>—THEN—UP AHEAD—LOOK ON THE LEFT OF THE TRAIL

SPECIAL HINT: Look for the huge boulder pointing to the sky like a bird looking up toward the sun. This rock formation looks like a bird head and beak! Use your imagination and find this rock bird!!!

_____**10 points**

#12 FIND THE LOW SHRUBS WITH SHARP-EDGED LEAVES!!! 15 STEPS PAST THE "BIG BIRD" BEAK—SEARCH ON THE LEFT OF THE TRAIL

SPECIAL HINT: This plant is called <u>dog-hobble</u> because it grows so tangled that pioneer dogs had trouble running through it as they chased after bears. The dogs would get stuck and hobble through these bushes! The bears, since they were bigger, stronger, and had protective fur on their stomachs could run right through! Rub your finger *gently* back and forth along the edge of a leaf. Your finger will let you know if it is dog-hobble!!!

_____**10 points**

#13 FIND THE QUARTZ "SANDWICH"!!! LOCATED ON THE OPPOSITE SIDE OF THE TRAIL FROM THE DOG-HOBBLE

SPECIAL HINT: Look for the rock with a strand of white <u>quartz</u> running right through it! Looks like a sandwich, eh? I bet it weighs more than a quarter pounder!!!

_____**10 points**

#14 LISTEN AND THEN FIND THE CASCADES AND WATERFALL THAT IS <u>*NOT*</u> GROTTO FALLS!!! CROSS A STREAM—SEARCH DOWN IN THE HOLLER ON THE LEFT

SPECIAL HINT: This is beautiful but is <u>not</u> the waterfall you are searching for! Keep going! You are almost there!!! The stream below you, <u>Roaring Fork</u>, is falling all the way from Mt. LeConte (over a mile high in elevation). It is likely the steepest stream in the Smoky Mountains! The water gets pretty noisy as it rushes down the mountain. Sounds kind of like a *"roar"!!!*

_____**10 points**

#15 FIND GROTTO FALLS!!! IN FRONT OF YOU

SPECIAL HINT: Listen for someone to say, "Whoa! Jiminy Crickets! Wow! There it is!!! (or something like that). There is a large pool at the base of the falls that is a perfect spot to cool off your feet on a hot day.

_____**10 points**

#16 WALK BEHIND GROTTO FALLS!!! CAREFULLY FOLLOW THE TRAIL THAT LEADS BEHIND THE FALLS

SPECIAL HINT: If you wish to get all wet, you will never have a better opportunity! This is called _Grotto_ Falls because of the cave-like opening behind the falls ("grotto" is another word for cave).

_____**10 points**

#17 FIND A SALAMANDER!!! LOOK AROUND THE BASE OF THE FALLS

SPECIAL HINT: Look under rocks and around the edges of the pool of water. Salamanders in the park grow 1/2-inch to over 2 feet long! There are over 30 different kinds of salamanders in all colors and sizes living in the park! Some folks call the Smokies the "Salamander Capital of the World!" Can you find just one? If you do find one, treat it gently and don't keep it out of the water for more than 1 minute. A salamander's skin can dry out very quickly!

_____**10 points**

CONGRATULATIONS!!!

YOU HAVE JUST COMPLETED A
GREAT SMOKY MOUNTAINS NATIONAL PARK

SCAVENGER HIKE ADVENTURE!!!

Trillium Gap Trail
to Grotto Falls

TEN POINTS FOR EACH ITEM FOUND

TOTAL SCORE _____

CERTIFIED ACHIEVEMENT

LEVEL_____

over 50 to 100 points: **City Slicker**
over 100 to 140 points: **Pioneer Scout**
over 140 points: **Frontier Explorer**

Name(s): _____

_____

Witness(es) thereof: _____

Date: _____

GREAT SMOKY MOUNTAINS

Scavenger Hike Adventure #6

<u>Big Creek Trail to Midnight Hole and Mouse Creek Falls</u>

<u>Why This Is a Great Trail!</u> This Scavenger Hike Adventure is located in Big Creek, an area of the park *off the beaten path.* If you want wilderness—O'brother, this is it! You will find some of the most awesome whitewater mountain stream views in the park! Someone very smart named this Big Creek because . . . this is a *really* big creek! On this trail, you will find boulders the size of *five* camping trailers stacked on top of each other!!! Find the huge Rock House up on a hill! Find the "Midnight Hole," a deep dark pool fed by beautiful cascading water squeezed between huge boulders! Sun yourself on the rocks, have a picnic, cool your feet in the water, and soak in the incredible beauty surrounding you! Mouse Creek Falls??? Give me a break! It is awesome!!! This trail is over an hour's drive from Gatlinburg, but the drive itself is *timeless* in mountain beauty found along the national park's Foothills Parkway and I-40. This hike is a hidden wilderness secret!

Where's the Trail? From Sugarlands Visitor Center head into Gatlinburg, north on Rt. 441. At **stoplight #3,** located just after the Hard Rock Café, bear right onto US 321 until you can't go any further (it comes to a T). Turn left at the "T" (toward I-40) and watch for the sign on the right that says "Foothills Parkway." Turn right and enjoy the 6-mile ride on the Foothills Parkway—mountain-view pull-offs are incredible!!!

Exit at I-40 east toward Asheville (another beautiful drive) and then take exit #451 (Waterville Road). Follow the sign to Big Creek. You'll travel alongside the Pigeon River and past the big hydro-electric plant.

After you pass <u>"Mountain Moma's" Appalachian Trail Hiker Stop</u> (hot showers, mail drop, and food place) continue through the intersection past the ranger station to the Big Creek picnic area and hikers' parking lot. By the way, Mountain Moma makes a great "Cheeseburger in Bearadise."

About the Trail: This trail is as wide as a road because it once *was* a road. It was originally an Indian path, then a logging road, and then a motor road to provide access for workers to build trails in the park. The trail is fairly level, sometimes rocky, and slopes gently up a ridge above Big Creek.

How Long Is This Hike? This Scavenger Hike Adventure is about 4 miles roundtrip. Allow about 2–3 hours, unless you take a nap and have a picnic on the rocks by "Midnight Hole." We would!

Things to Hunt For
(Earn 10 points for each treasure you find)

#1 FIND THE REMAINS OF AN OLD LOGGING MILL!!!
LOCATED IN THE PICNIC AREA AND HIKERS' PARKING LOT

SPECIAL HINT: Find the mill's red brick foundation with many steel bars sticking up from the base! Can you believe that you are standing in the middle of what was once a busy logging community called Crestmont??? There was a passenger railroad station, a general store with a soda fountain, and a logging mill. In the early 1900s the loggers cut down most of the trees in this area and now new trees have grown back. That is why it is called a "second-growth" forest.

_____10 points

#2 FIND THE SPECIAL BEAR-PROOF GARBAGE CAN!!!
LOCATED IN THE PARKING LOT

SPECIAL HINT: There are about 2,000 black bears in the park! This special garbage can is built so that a bear *can't* put his paw in it to get food. Check it out! If bears eat people food, they'll get into trouble looking for food in all the wrong places! *Never* feed a bear, because he will lose his wild instincts and become "habituated," which means he loses his fear of people. That is not a good thing for him or us!!! Bears that are not afraid of humans may become "nuisance" bears and often have to be removed from the park or sometimes killed. *So please don't feed the bears!!!*

_____10 points

#3 FIND THE FURRY VINE CLIMBING UP THE "TRIPLET" TULIP TREE!!! AT THE CORNER OF THE PARKING AREA NEAR A HUGE SAWED-OFF TREE TRUNK

SPECIAL HINT: This tulip tree is joined at the bottom but then splits into three trunks and looks sort of like a "triplet" tree. The furry vine climbing up the tree is poison ivy! Poison ivy has groups of three leaves and grows on the ground, but occasionally just attaches to a tree and heads to the sky! Leaves of three . . . leave me be! Furry vine . . . itch and whine! Do not touch the vine or the leaves. Hiking and itching like crazy at the same time is not a good thing! You'll see a few more huge furry poison ivy vines on the left as you head up the trail.

_____**10 points**

#4 FIND THE CHRISTMAS FERNS!!! ON THE RIGHT— NEAR THE BEGINNING OF THE TRAIL

SPECIAL HINT: The folks that named this evergreen fern thought that the individual leaves were shaped like Santa's sleigh or maybe a Christmas stocking. What do you think??? If you're hiking in December, "Merry Christmas!!!"

_____**10 points**

#5 FIND HUNDREDS OF PENCIL TREES!!! ON THE LEFT
AS YOU LOOK TOWARD THE CREEK

SPECIAL HINT: As you continue on the trail and look to the left, you can't help but notice the hundreds of extremely tall and straight tulip trees (also called yellow poplar). They look like giant pencils! This area was cleared by loggers in the early 1900s and with all the trees gone, the sun shined brightly down below you and the tulip tree seedlings absolutely loved it! You are looking at a huge "stand" of tulip trees. Throughout the park when you see a group of trees like this it indicates that the land was probably once cleared either by loggers or farmers.

_____**10 points**

#6 FIND THE AWESOME LOOKING STRATIFIED SANDSTONE FORMATION!!! ON THE MOUNTAINSIDE—ON THE
RIGHT OF THE TRAIL—AFTER YOU SEE THE CREEK FLOWING CLOSE BY THE TRAIL—START LOOKING

SPECIAL HINT: Some of the rocks look like shingles sticking out from the side of the mountain. The thin layers of rock sometimes rise about 50 feet along this trail! Just look for the layered rocks that run along the trail for about a quarter of a mile. It is quite awesome!

_____**10 points**

#7 FIND AMAZING TREES GROWING RIGHT OUT OF A BOULDER THE SIZE OF A SCHOOL BUS!!! LOOK UP AND INTO THE FOREST ON THE RIGHT

SPECIAL HINT: There are three trees growing out of a boulder the size of a school bus!!!

_____**10 points**

#8 FIND THOUSANDS OF HUGE BOULDERS STREWN ON THE MOUNTAINSIDE!!! HIKE 10 TO 15 MINUTES—SEARCH ON THE RIGHT SIDE OF THE TRAIL ON THE SIDE OF THE MOUNTAIN

SPECIAL HINT: Due to freezing and thawing, these rocks cracked and broke off from the mountain and then tumbled on down! Geologists call large groups of boulders, such as you see here, a "<u>block field</u>." You'll see thousands of boulders in this block field! Scientists believe some rocks in the Smokies are about 600 million years old. The boulders on this trail are so huge and awesome that when you see them they just might knock your hiking socks off!!! If you are not sure that you have found the block field . . . *you haven't!*

_____**10 points**

#9 FIND A BOULDER AS BIG AS A WINNEBAGO!!! ON THE RIGHT SIDE OF THE TRAIL—YOU COULD TOUCH IT WITH A HIKING STICK WITHOUT STEPPING OFF THE TRAIL

SPECIAL HINT: If this had wheels, windows, and an engine you could use it as an RV!!!

_____**10 points**

#10 FIND THE ROCK HOUSE IN THE SKY!!!

ON THE RIGHT SIDE OF THE TRAIL—WAY UP HIGH
AMONG THE TREES—START LOOKING WHEN BIG
CREEK GETS VERY CLOSE TO THE TRAIL AND YOU
SEE A LOT OF BOULDERS THE SIZE OF SMALL CARS IN THE CREEK

      SPECIAL HINT: This is likely the most unusual boulder you've ever seen in your life!!! You have seen some *huge* boulders on this trail but *this one is at least twice as big* as the biggest one you've seen so far!!! It <u>looks more like a house than a boulder</u>! A <u>narrow, steep, almost hidden footpath</u> leads up to the Rock House! It has three walls and a ceiling and loggers would use it to get in out of bad weather.

_____**10 points**

#11 FIND THE WALL OF RHODODENDRON BUSHES!!!
LOCATED ON THE RIGHT SIDE OF THE TRAIL—ALL ALONG THE WAY

SPECIAL HINT: The leaves of these plants are long and slender and are green year round. The leaves are really thick and feel like leather. They are full of beautiful blossoms in the summer. Cherokee Indians once lived in this area. They *would not burn* rhododendron wood or leaves because they believed it would bring cold winter weather. The burning wood and leaves would hiss and sound like a windy snowstorm!

_____**10 points**

#12 FIND THE AWESOME "MIDNIGHT HOLE!!!" HIKE
AWHILE—LOOK ON THE LEFT SIDE OF THE TRAIL DOWN IN THE CREEK WHEN YOU FIND A <u>WIDE OPEN ROCKY CLEARING</u>

SPECIAL HINT: As you walk along, look for a dark deep pool of water fed by waterfalls that rush <u>between large boulders</u> in the middle of the creek. When the water is high there will be one waterfall and when the water is lower you will see two waterfalls plummeting over the rocks. There is a wide opening and a well-worn path leading down to the Midnight Hole. The pool is dark green in the winter and midnight blue in the summer. This is an awesome spot for sunning and picnicking! Take off your shoes and rest a spell! It doesn't get any better than this!!!

_____**10 points**

#13 FIND A TROUT!!! IN THE MIDNIGHT HOLE

SPECIAL HINT: Trout like to hang out in the Midnight Hole. Look carefully and you may be able to spot one. There are 2,000 to 4,000 trout per mile in some of the streams in the park! During the middle of the day, trout usually rest near the bottom so cup your eyes and peer deeply into the hole. One local old-timer comes up here every week to fish for a couple of meals!

_____**10 points**

#14 FIND THE ROCK WALL THAT HOLDS UP THE TRAIL!!!
NEAR THE MIDNIGHT HOLE—ALONGSIDE THE TRAIL

SPECIAL HINT: As you return to the trail from the Midnight Hole, look for the rock wall that supports the trail. Big Creek Trail was once an Indian path! In the early 1900s loggers used the trail as a logging road! In the 1930s it became an automobile road for the men who were building the trails in the park! Now, Big Creek Trail is a hiking trail for people and horses!

_____10 points

#15 FIND THE HUMONGOUS BOULDER THAT LOOKS LIKE A HOUSE WITH A GREEN ROOF AND GREEN TRIM!!! ON THE RIGHT SIDE OF THE TRAIL—BEHIND SOME RHODODENDRON BUSHES

SPECIAL HINT: This boulder stands alone and is about the size of a two-story house! This giant "pebble" is covered with soft green moss! It almost looks like a house with a green roof!

_____10 points

60

#16 FIND THE HITCHING POSTS FOR HORSES!!! ON THE LEFT SIDE OF THE TRAIL—NEAR A WIDE-OPEN AREA

SPECIAL HINT: Tie up your horses (or anyone who said, "Are we almost there yet?") and mosey on over to Mouse Creek Falls!

_____**10 points**

#17 FIND MOUSE CREEK FALLS!!! JUST A FEW FEET UPSTREAM FROM THE HITCHING POSTS

SPECIAL HINT: Find the beautiful cascading waterfall that drops 50 feet to Mouse Creek!!! There used to be railroad tracks used for logging at the base of the falls. The railroad line was located right where the water first hits the flat area. Listen! You *won't* hear the sound of a train engine chugging along with black smoke pumping out of the stack. Today, you will only hear the peaceful sounds of nature as the crystal clear mountain water tumbles from the high slopes of Mt. Sterling.

_____**10 points**

Bonus Courtesy Hint: If you didn't find the Rock House and want to try *one more time*—it is located about 550 steps heading back from the side path leading to <u>Midnight Hole</u>.

CONGRATULATIONS!!!

YOU HAVE JUST COMPLETED A
GREAT SMOKY MOUNTAINS NATIONAL PARK

SCAVENGER HIKE ADVENTURE!!!

<u>Big Creek Trail to Midnight Hole</u>
<u>and Mouse Creek Falls</u>

TEN POINTS FOR EACH ITEM
FOUND

TOTAL SCORE _____

CERTIFIED ACHIEVEMENT
LEVEL_____

over 50 to 100 points: <u>City Slicker</u>
over 100 to 140 points: <u>Pioneer Scout</u>
over 140 points: <u>Frontier Explorer</u>

Name(s): _____

_____

Witness(es) thereof: _____

Date: _____

GREAT SMOKY MOUNTAINS

Scavenger Hike Adventure #7

Sugarlands Valley Nature Trail

Why This Is a Great Trail! This is an *easy and exciting* Scavenger Hike Adventure through a deep green forest along a beautiful mountain stream! You will find the actual footpath Cherokee Indians walked on to get to North Carolina a long long time ago! A whole community of pioneers lived in this *Sugarlands* area, which was named for all of the sugar maple trees that used to be here! One thing for sure, these pioneers had *plenty* of maple syrup! A black bear liked this trail so much he couldn't *bear* to wait for the wet cement to dry! Find the paw prints! Be cool! You can dip your feet in a mountain stream! This trail is great for everyone!!!

Where's the Trail? From the Sugarlands Visitor Center (an awesome place to visit!!!) this trail is about a 2 minute (less than a half-mile) drive south on Rt. 441 toward Cherokee, North Carolina, and Newfound Gap. It is *so close* there is not even time for anyone to ask, "Are we there yet?" Look on the right side of the road for the sign "Sugarlands Valley Nature Trail." Parking and the trail will be on the left.

About the Trail: This paved trail is wide and level and great for wheelchairs and strollers. It is almost totally shaded because it goes through a thick forest. There are also *many* benches to relax on along the way!

How Long Is This Hike? This Scavenger Hike Adventure is about a 1/2-mile loop and will take less than an hour to complete!

Things to Hunt For
(Earn 10 points for each treasure you find)

#1 FIND A BIG ROCK WITH TWO HOLES SHAPED LIKE EYES!!! ON THE RIGHT—NEAR START OF THE TRAIL

SPECIAL HINT: Use your imagination! Does it look like anyone in *your* family? How did nature make those holes? Most likely these holes were made by water swirling on the rock for millions of years! Swirling waters can make rocks round and smooth like this one. Fast-moving streams carry stones, logs, and grains of sand that can make cracks, holes, and marks on the rocks. This rock isn't quite ready to be placed on Mt. Rushmore, but it *is* an interesting "face"!

_____**10 points**

#2 FIND A TREE THAT LOOKS MORE LIKE A "TWIN" TREE!!! ABOUT TEN STEPS BEFORE REACHING THE FOOTBRIDGE— ON THE RIGHT OF THE TRAIL

SPECIAL HINT: Nature is *amazing!!!* The trunk of this tree was somehow split and has grown into *two* trunks! When this tree was very young it definitely experienced some sort of trauma! Maybe it was struck by lightning, chewed on by an animal, or damaged by strong winds. *Something* caused the trunk to grow into "twin twunks" and to grow into what now looks like a "twin twee"!!!

_____**10 points**

#3 FIND THE NUMBER OF FAMILIES THAT ONCE LIVED IN THE SUGARLANDS VALLEY!!! AT MARKER #1

SPECIAL HINT: Check out this sign! Indians walked on this land prior to white settlers! Pioneers came here over 150 years ago and life was not easy for them! They had to work hard to survive! The Smoky Mountains is a very *rocky* place and pioneers had to move thousands of heavy rocks to clear this land so they could plant crops and raise their own animals for food! Where you are now standing was once a community with three schools, a post office, two churches, two tub mills, a saw mill, farm fields, and many homesteads! Just think, people lived here even when Abraham Lincoln was president!!!

_____**10 points**

65

#4 FIND A LARGE STONE CHIMNEY AND A FIREPLACE WITH ONLY HALF OF A MANTLE!!! ON THE LEFT OF THE TRAIL

SPECIAL HINT: This fireplace and chimney was built about 100 years ago! What you see is all that is left of a family's summer vacation home! People built vacation homes in the Smokies as early as 1900. In the early 1930s, Congress decided to make the Smoky Mountains into a national park so all the land in this area was bought from private owners. Imagine sitting by this fireplace way back then! People loved to vacation in the Smokies! I guess *some* things *never* change!!!

_____**10 points**

#5 SPOT A ROCK (BOULDER) THAT WEIGHS MORE THAN YOU!!! ON THE LEFT OF THE TRAIL—RIGHT PAST THE BENCH—DOWN IN THE STREAM

SPECIAL HINT: There are lots of humongous and very heavy boulders in the Smoky Mountains! How in the world did all of these huge rocks get here? At one time the Smoky Mountains were much higher than they are today! These mountains were even taller than the Rocky Mountains! During a much colder era, water froze in cracks in the mountain rock. When it froze, it expanded and broke the rock! Gravity and fast-moving rivers and streams then carried these huge boulders down the mountains to where they are today!!! In the Smokies there are boulders, boulders, everywhere!!!

_____**10 points**

#6 FIND THE REMAINS OF ANOTHER SMOKY MOUNTAIN VACATION HOME!!! ON THE RIGHT OF THE TRAIL

SPECIAL HINT: This fireplace has white <u>quartz</u> rocks built into the front of the stone work. We'll never know why the builder decided to put them there. Maybe the stones had some special meaning to him. Take a look! Quartz is a very common rock in the Smokies and is often milky white.

_____**10 points**

#7 FIND THE SOFT BEAUTIFUL HEMLOCK TREES!!!
SURROUNDING THE CHIMNEY AND FIREPLACE

SPECIAL HINT: Hemlock trees have short flat needles. Some describe these beautiful branches of needles as "lacy." Hemlocks have very tiny cones. Gently rub the needles between your fingers and take a "whiff." Now, when someone asks "What did you do today?" say "I smelled a hemlock!!!" A tiny insect from Asia called the hemlock wooly adelgid ("a-del-jid") is attacking our hemlocks. Park rangers are doing all that they can do to save these beautiful trees.

_____**10 points**

#8 FIND UMBRELLAS OVER YOUR HEAD!!! ABOUT 46 STEPS
PAST THE CHIMNEY

SPECIAL HINT: Look straight up! Find the leaves of the umbrella magnolia tree! Umbrellas sure come in handy in the Smokies because it rains *a lot* here! It rains more in the Smokies than in almost any other place in the United States!!! In fact, it rains more than 7 feet each year in the higher elevations! This is one of the reasons why the Smokies is such a special place! There are "zillions" of plants and animals that live here! There are more kinds of trees than in any other area of the same size in the whole United States! There are more flowering plants than in any other national park in our country! The *diversity* of life in the Smokies is incredible!!! (Umbrellas are not available in winter and early spring.)

_____**10 points**

#9 FIND A TREE THAT LOOKS LIKE IT'S WEARING A SHOE!!! ON THE LEFT OF THE TRAIL—PAST THE BENCH

SPECIAL HINT: This tree trunk looks just like a very long leg that is wearing a shoe made of rock! Nature has a great sense of humor!!!

_____**10 points**

#10 FIND THE OLD CHEROKEE INDIAN FOOTPATH!!! AT MARKER #3—IN THE GULLY—NEAR THE STREAM

SPECIAL HINT: Stand in the <u>gully</u> between Marker #3 and the stream! You are actually standing on an old Indian path where Cherokee Indians walked all the way to North Carolina many years ago! Imagine Indians walking down this foot-path! Many Cherokee Indians lived in the area of the Smoky Mountains long ago and many <u>still</u> live across the mountains in Cherokee, North Carolina, on the Qualla Indian Reservation!!!

_____**10 points**

#11 LISTEN FOR THE MUSIC OF THE WATER!!! STAND OR SIT BY THE STREAM

SPECIAL HINT: Listen for the sounds of the rushing water. Which sounds do you hear? (Kerplunk??? Gurgle???? Galump??? Whooooosh?????) The sounds of the water can also be very soothing! Many fish make this beautiful stream their home. The only native trout in the Smokies is the brook trout. Brown and rainbow trout were stocked in the Smokies years ago. Of course, the fish are protected in this park, but as long as you follow the park fishing regulations you can "go fish"!!!

_____**10 points**

#12 FIND AN OLD ROCK WALL!!! ON BOTH SIDES OF THE TRAIL

SPECIAL HINT: Wow!!! Lots of heavy rocks make up this wall! Early settlers built these walls when they had to clear the land so they could plant crops, raise animals, and build cabins. This was very hard work! Remember, much of this area was cornfields in the pioneer days. Perhaps this wall kept cows from eating the corn that mountain folks needed for their meals. Pioneer children helped build these big heavy walls!!!

_____10 points

#13 FIND BLACK BEAR PAW PRINTS IN THE CEMENT!!! GO PAST THREE BENCHES—THEN FIND A SIGN ON THE RIGHT THAT MARKS THE SPOT—LOOK DOWN

SPECIAL HINT: Look closely! You can find bear prints in the concrete!!! I guess this bear just couldn't wait for the concrete to dry before he crossed the trail! There are about 2,000 black bears living in the park and you might find one *any-where!* Can you believe a "mama" bear actually gives birth to her cubs in the winter while she is asleep! Amazing!!! Bears like to nap high in the tree tops. They are great climbers! Simon says, "Look up!"

_____10 points

#14 FIND A TREE THAT LOOKS LIKE A PRETZEL!!! ON THE LEFT OF THE TRAIL—ACROSS FROM THE BENCH—LOOK UP

SPECIAL HINT: Look up high and see two branches of a tree that are twisted together almost like a pretzel! Winds can twist these branches every which way!!!

_____10 points

#15 FIND A GROOVY TREE!!!—ON THE RIGHT OF THE TRAIL—AFTER A SHARP 90-DEGREE TURN —AFTER THE BENCH—NEXT TO A SIGN

SPECIAL HINT: This sign says this tree is a <u>sourwood</u> tree! You can put your fingers in the grooves of this tree's thick bark! The bark almost looks like the tread on the tires of your car. Mountain folks seldom chopped down sourwood trees to use for fuel because they loved the honey the bees made from it's flowers! You can buy sourwood honey in town. Try it! You'll like it!!!

_____**10 points**

#16 FIND THE BABY BIRDS WITH A MOTHER BIRD!!!
WALK A WHILE—ON THE RIGHT SIDE OF THE TRAIL

SPECIAL HINT: Look closely and see how many baby birds are waiting to be fed by their mother! Indians, pioneers, vacationers, and lots of critters have all come to the Sugarlands Valley. Many animals now make the Smokies their home! In the Smokies, birds are more often heard than seen because they are hidden in the thick forests of trees and plants. The Great Smoky Mountains National Park has over 230 species of birds! The largest bird that lives here is the wild turkey! Hope you see one! It is an awesome bird!!!

_____**10 points**

#17 FIND THE DOG-HOBBLE!!! ON LEFT OF THE TRAIL—ACROSS FROM MARKER #5

SPECIAL HINT: This low evergreen plant has sharp edges on its leaves. Rub your finger gently back and forth across the edge of a leaf! These tangled bushes are called "dog-hobble." A long time ago, dogs would get tangled up in these low bushes while they were chasing after bears. I guess you could say these bushes could really make a dog hobble! The bigger, stronger bears would just glide right through the dog-hobble! Dog-hobble lives only in the southern Appalachian mountains. Some of the leaves turn bronze, maroon, and copper in the fall and winter.

_____**10 points**

#18 FIND POISON IVY CLIMBING UP A TREE!!!

15 STEPS BACK TOWARD THE START OF THE TRAIL FROM THE "POISON IVY" SIGN—ON THE RIGHT OF THE TRAIL AS YOU RETRACE YOUR STEPS BACK

SPECIAL HINT: This furry vine is poison ivy! Don't touch it! It will make you itch! Poison ivy can also come in the form of three green leaves. Remember! Leaves of three—let them be!!! Furry vine—you'll itch and whine!!! It is not uncommon to find poison ivy vines as thick as your arm climbing up the sides of large trees here in the Smokies!!!

_____**10 points**

#19 JUST FOR FUN! FIND THE OLDEST PERSON IN YOUR GROUP AND SPEAK TO HIM OR HER IN CHEROKEE!!!

SPECIAL HINT: Say **"Shee-oh. Doh-huh-dun-nay?"** This is Cherokee for "Hi! How are you doing?" Chief Sequoyah first discovered that the spoken word could also be written down when he saw white settlers reading from a printed paper. He called the paper with words "talking leaves." Chief Sequoya wanted his people to have "talking leaves" so he spent the next 12 years writing symbols for each Cherokee syllable. *On his own* he developed the written Cherokee language. Today, children in Cherokee, North Carolina, learn both the English and the Cherokee language in their schools.

_____**10 points**

71

#20 FIND A TULIP TREE!!! ON THE RIGHT OF THE TRAIL—ABOUT 42 STEPS PAST MARKER #6—SEARCH ON THE RIGHT OF THE TRAIL—A SIGN MARKS THE SPOT

SPECIAL HINT: Look straight up!!! Today this forest is made up of many very tall tulip trees. A tulip tree is often a sign of where a cornfield used to be. Tulip trees grow up in sunny places and since this area was once an open field and was also logged there was certainly lots of sun! Tulip trees, also known as yellow poplar trees, were often *so large* that a pioneer family could build a whole cabin from *just one* tree!!!

_____**10 points**

#21 FIND THE PANCAKE SYRUP TREE!!! 28 STEPS FROM THE TULIP TREE—ON THE RIGHT

SPECIAL HINT: Pioneers used the sap from the sugar maple tree to make delicious maple syrup. Pass the pancakes please!!!

_____**10 points**

CONGRATULATIONS!!!

YOU HAVE JUST COMPLETED A
GREAT SMOKY MOUNTAINS NATIONAL PARK

SCAVENGER HIKE ADVENTURE!!!

<u>Sugarlands Valley</u>
<u>Nature Trail</u>

TEN POINTS FOR EACH ITEM FOUND

TOTAL SCORE _____

CERTIFIED ACHIEVEMENT

LEVEL_____

over 50 to 100 points: <u>**City Slicker**</u>
over 100 to 180 points: <u>**Pioneer Scout**</u>
over 180 points: <u>**Frontier Explorer**</u>

Name(s): _____

_____

Witness(es) thereof: _____

Date: _____

GREAT SMOKY MOUNTAINS

Scavenger Hike Adventure #8

<u>Cades Cove to Abrams Falls Trail
to Abrams Falls</u>

<u>Why This Is a Great Trail!</u> This Scavenger Hike Adventure begins in world famous Cade's Cove with a search for deer and bears on the way to the trailhead! Cade's Cove is a beautiful valley surrounded by majestic mountains. Can you believe one visitor saw 200 deer on just *one* trip through Cade's Cove!!! There have also been hundreds of sightings of bears up in cherry trees or meandering through these woods. This hiking trail follows Abrams Creek, the *biggest* stream that runs entirely within the boundaries of the park. You'll find a gargantuan white pine tree, the most hypnotic smooth cascade you've ever seen, more mountain laurel than you can shake a stick at, and finally powerful Abrams Falls crashing 25 feet into a huge deep pool of water! This is a great place to cool off and picnic!

Where's the Trail? At Sugarland's Visitor Center follow the signs to Cade's Cove. It's about 24 miles (about an hour's drive) on beautiful winding Little River Road. Then follow the Cade's Cove loop road for about 5 miles and turn right (just past marker #10) onto the gravel road following the sign to the Abrams Falls trailhead.

About the Trail: This is a wide and mostly level trail, but has three or four pretty good hills to climb. The trail is sometimes dirt and pine needles, sometimes very rocky, and sometimes very "rooty." The trail runs along Abrams Creek the entire journey to the falls. This is a moderately difficult trail, but is a very popular family hike.

How Long Is This Hike? This Scavenger Hike Adventure is 5 miles roundtrip. You should allow 3–4 hours.

Special Comment: Cades Cove has a one-way 11-mile road that loops around the valley. The trailhead is located about half-way around the big loop. Before you head out on the loop, you might want to stop at the campground store to get a sandwich or an ice cream cone! Traffic on the loop often comes to a standstill when a visitor sees a bear and locals call that a "bear jam." You won't be able to hurry around the loop. Oh, by the way, have we mentioned that this road is a loop? Remember though, *the journey is the destination*.

Things to Hunt For
(Earn 10 points for each treasure you find)

#1 FIND A DEER!!! AS YOU ENTER THE CADES COVE LOOP—GO ON TO #2 AS YOU SEARCH

SPECIAL HINT: You have 5 miles to spot a deer before you get to the Abrams Falls trailhead. Ready . . . Set . . . Go!!!

_____10 points

#2 FIND A BLACK BEAR!!! AS YOU DRIVE ALONG THE CADES COVE LOOP—GO ON TO #3 AS YOU SEARCH

SPECIAL HINT: After you find a deer, search for a black bear! Don't forget to look up in trees and deep into the woods. There are about 2,000 bears in this park. A black bear weighs less than a can of soda at birth and can grow to over 400 pounds. Try to find *just* one. ***Never approach a bear. Keep your distance!!!***

_____10 points

#3 FIND A WILD TURKEY!!! ON THE WAY TO THE TRAILHEAD

SPECIAL HINT: While you're searching for a bear and a deer, you may as well keep your eye out for the biggest bird in the park. In the spring, male wild turkeys can be heard gobbling from a mile away. Roll your window down!

_____**10 points**

#4 FIND THE SITE OF JOHN OLIVER'S GUEST LODGE!!!
JUST BEFORE REACHING THE FOOTBRIDGE AT THE TRAILHEAD

SPECIAL HINT: Look for the large grouping of hemlock trees (short needles about as long as your fingernail). Gently rub the needles of the tree between your thumb and fingers and then take a whiff. Now, the next time someone asks if you have ever really smelled a hemlock tree say, **"Uh"** (Cherokee for "yes") and then say, **"Zee-yookt guh-noh-hee-ahay"** (Cherokee for "I speak the truth.") Cherokee Indians lived in the Cade's Cove area and Abrams Falls is named after <u>Cherokee Chief Abram</u>. By the way, John Oliver's guest lodge stood right here about 80 years ago. He was the great-grandson of the first white settler, also named John Oliver, who came to Cades Cove in the fall of 1818.

_____**10 points**

#5 FIND THE "THERMOMETER" JUNGLE!!! AFTER YOU CROSS THE FOOTBRIDGE

SPECIAL HINT: Search for an evergreen plant with very long narrow and thick leaves. Its flowers bloom in the summer. Pioneers used these leaves as "thermometers." When the leaves darken and droop, it is about 32 degrees. At around 20 degrees the leaves curl and roll up. At 0 degrees, the leaves roll up as tight as a pencil. How cool is that? By the way, the Cherokees would put a leaf on their forehead to heal a headache. They didn't have Advil back then. *Remember to never ever pick a leaf or damage any plant life. Each plant is protected by our national park!!!*

_____**10 points**

#6 FIND A SIGN OF A BEAR!!! SEARCH ALL ALONG THE TRAIL TO THE FALLS—GO ON TO #7 AS YOU KEEP YOUR EYES WIDE OPEN

SPECIAL HINT: Look for dead logs and trees that were clawed open or shredded by bears looking for grubs and other critter snacks. There are a lot of signs of bears along this trail. Hmmmmm!!! When cold weather is just around the corner, bears in the Smokies often find a hollow tree high above the ground to sleep in for the winter.

_____**10 points**

#7 FIND A LIVING CREATURE IN THE STREAM!!! BETWEEN HERE AND THE FALLS STOP BY THE STREAM AND TAKE A CLOSE LOOK

SPECIAL HINT: Years ago river otters were abundant here. In fact, the Cherokee Indians once called this area, **"Tsiyahai,"** meaning "place of the otter." The otters were trapped for their fur and became extinct in the park. In 1986 the park reintroduced river otters into the Abrams Creek area. Who knows? Maybe you'll find a river otter, a fish, a water strider (looks like a floating spider with only 6 legs), a salamander, or a snake!!!

_____**10 points**

#8 FIND THE GARGANTUAN (GIANT) WHITE PINE TREE!!!

WALK QUITE A WAYS—THIS TREE IS <u>ON</u> THE LEFT EDGE OF THE TRAIL

SPECIAL HINT: You'll walk quite a ways before you find this giant of the forest. You will pass several large trees, but when you reach this tree you will say, "That has got to be it!" It has reddish-brown thick bark with deep furrows and <u>two normal-sized pioneers arm to arm could not encircle this tree trunk!!!</u> Key hint: It is located just <u>on the edge of</u> the trail. To be sure you found the right tree, find a deep hole at the base of this giant tree trunk. Also, the long needles come in bunches of five.

_____**10 points**

#9 FIND THE GALAX!!! (PRONOUNCED GAY-LAX) 92 STEPS

PAST THE GIANT WHITE PINE— LOOK ON THE RIGHT SIDE OF TRAIL — ON THE SIDE OF THE HILL

SPECIAL HINT: This is a very *shiny* evergreen plant that grows low to the ground and its leaves are kind of circular or perhaps like a "fat" heartshape. Galax grows only in the southern Appalachian Mountains. It blooms a pillar of tiny white flowers in the summer and they smell like *garlic*. Mountain people would gather galax, which turns crimson in the fall, and sell it to florists who would use it in bouquets and other floral arrangements. *Remember, never pick anything or take anything from the park!*

_____**10 points**

#10 FIND THE NATURAL ROCK SEAT AND STAIRWAY!!!

AT THE TOP OF THE HILL

SPECIAL HINT: When you reach the top of the ridge, look to your right for a tree that grew right through a rock. There are so many rocks and such little soil that this tree's roots are searching every which way for food and water. The rock seat is right below that tree and the stairway (rocks) lead down the hill at that point. In the spring the seat is totally surrounded by a bouquet of beautiful mountain laurel. Definitely a photo-op!!!

_____**10 points**

#11 FIND THE LAUREL HELL!!! LOCATED JUST BEFORE THE LOG FOOTBRIDGE

SPECIAL HINT: The pioneers called this tangled quagmire of rhododendron plants a "laurel hell" because it was very hard to walk through. Back then rhododendron was called "laurel." Imagine you and your family trying to get to Aunt Lucinda's cabin through this thicket!!!

_____**10 points**

#12 FIND THE WHITEWATER CASCADE!!! COUNT 70 STEPS AFTER YOU CROSS THE LOG FOOTBRIDGE

SPECIAL HINT: Look in the creek at the water flowing over the rocks. This is called a cascade. Hope you have at least one more shot left on your camera!!!

_____**10 points**

#13 FIND THE YELLOW LICHEN ON THE ROCKS!!! YOU WILL HIKE FOR QUITE AWHILE—LOCATED NEAR THE TOP OF THE *NEXT* HILL—ON THE RIGHT—ON THE ROCKS

SPECIAL HINT: The trail is level for quite a ways before you reach the next steep hill. This lichen (pronounced "like-in") is growing on the rocks and looks like bright yellow spray paint! Lichen is a combination of <u>algae and fungus</u>. The acid in lichen gradually eats away at the rock, breaking it into very tiny particles which eventually become soil. If you come to the hairpin-curve that goes to the right, you are 40 steps <u>past</u> the lichen!!!

_____**10 points**

#14 FIND THE DOG-HOBBLE!!! LOCATED ABOUT 12 STEPS FROM THE MIDDLE POINT OF THE GIANT U-TURN

SPECIAL HINT: As you go down the long steep hill, you will pass an empty stump and see the perfect U-turn in the trail down below. The only way to tell for sure if you have found the dog-hobble is to run your finger back and forth along the edge of a leaf. If you can feel the jagged edges you have found it!!! Dogs would get stuck or hobbled in these bushes as they chased after bears and that's why the mountain folks called it dog-hobble. Dog-hobble only grows in the southern Appalachian Mountains. This means that dogs in Chicago and other major metropolitan regions don't have to worry about it!!!

_____**10 points**

#15 FIND THE TREE WITH A BAD "ROOT" DAY!!! CROSS A LOG FOOTBRIDGE—WALK QUITE AWHILE—GO UP A LONG HILL

SPECIAL HINT: You'll see many roots along the way, but these are the only roots that form a "rooty" seat. Need a break? Sit on a root! You actually have to walk around these wacky tree roots to stay on the trail! Have you ever had a bad "hair" day? Well, it looks like this tree is having a bad "root" day!!!

_____**10 points**

#16 FIND THE WARNING SIGN!!! ON THE LEFT—AT THE TOP OF THE HILL

SPECIAL HINT: Abrams Falls is a powerful waterfall and one of the slipperiest areas in the park. This warning sign is here for a reason. ***Be extremely careful around the falls!!!***

_____10 points

#17 FIND THE SMOOTHEST HYPNOTIC CASCADE YOU'VE EVER SEEN!!! JUST BEFORE YOU REACH THE LOG FOOTBRIDGE— BEFORE THE FALLS

SPECIAL HINT: The water just seems to magically glide over the rocks. This cascade is almost hypnotic in beauty!!!

_____10 points

#18 FIND ABRAMS FALLS AND THE AWESOME DEEP POOL!!! YOU MADE IT!!!

SPECIAL HINT: Relax, take a break, have a snack, take a nap, read a book, take a look, you must be beat, dangle your feet, take a sip, eat a chip! Enjoy it. You deserve it!!!

_____10 points

#19 FIND ELIJAH OLIVER'S CABIN!!! LOOK FOR A SIGN
BEFORE YOU REACH THE FOOTBRIDGE NEAR THE START OF THE TRAIL

SPECIAL HINT: You can find Elijah Oliver's cabin, smokehouse, stable, springhouse, corncrib, barn and small cabin guest room by walking 1/2 mile down the side trail. Too tired? Then check out his cabin on the cover of <u>Scavenger Hike Adventures</u>! Elijah was the son of the first white settler in Cades Cove, John Oliver. What's cool about this cabin is the little room that he built right on the front porch. It was used for guests and was called the "stranger room." Give yourself 20 points if you hike to the actual cabin or 10 points if you just find it on the cover of this book!!!

_____**10 points**

CONGRATULATIONS!!!

YOU HAVE JUST COMPLETED A
GREAT SMOKY MOUNTAINS NATIONAL PARK

SCAVENGER HIKE ADVENTURE!!!

<u>Cades Cove to Abrams Falls Trail</u>
<u>to Abrams Falls</u>

TEN POINTS FOR EACH ITEM FOUND

TOTAL SCORE _____ (20 points for hiking to Elijah Oliver's Cabin or 10 points if you just find it on the book cover)

CERTIFIED ACHIEVEMENT

LEVEL_____

over 50 to 100 points: <u>**City Slicker**</u>
over 100 to 140 points: <u>**Pioneer Scout**</u>
over 140 points: <u>**Frontier Explorer**</u>

Name(s): _____

_____

Witness(es) thereof: _____

Date:_____

GREAT SMOKY MOUNTAINS

Scavenger Hike Adventure #9

Fighting Creek Nature Trail

Why This Is a Great Trail! On this Scavenger Hike Adventure we *guarantee* that you will see a black bear, a wild turkey, a red-cheeked salamander (that lives only in the Smokies and nowhere else on earth!) a white-tailed deer, and a wild hog!!! You will walk a mile in the moccasins of Cherokee Indians who hunted and maybe even farmed in this area! In the middle 1800s there was a community of settlers that lived here. This community was called "Forks of the River." Back then there were about 25 farmsteads in "Forks of the River"! You will find the authentic log cabin of pioneer John Ownby and his old-time "refrigerator!" You will find the strangest sycamore tree that you will ever see in your lifetime! If that's not enough, you'll find a cornfield that a pioneer almost fell out of!!!

Where's the Trail? From the Sugarlands Visitor Center simply follow the path that leads behind the building and you will see a sign for the Fighting Creek Nature Trail.

About the Trail: This Scavenger Hike Adventure is on a trail that is a bit hilly, but even an inexperienced small pioneer can handle it! There are also benches along the way to take an occasional break. The trail is wide enough for two pioneers to walk side by side. You'll walk alongside and across Fighting Creek!!!

How Long Is This Hike? This Scavenger Hike Adventure is a bit less than a mile roundtrip and will take about an hour to complete. It starts behind the Sugarlands Visitor Center and loops back to the same point.

Things to Hunt For
(Earn 10 points for each treasure you find)

#1 FIND A BLACK BEAR, A WILD TURKEY, A WHITE-TAILED DEER, A WILD HOG, AND A RED-CHEEKED SALAMANDER (ONLY FOUND IN THE SMOKIES AND NOWHERE ELSE ON EARTH!) YOU MIGHT FIND <u>SOME</u> OF THESE ANIMALS ALONG THE TRAIL, BUT . . .

SPECIAL HINT: You'll be <u>*sure*</u> to find them in the Sugarlands Visitor Center! It's a great place. Don't miss it!!!

_____10 points

#2 FIND THE CORNFIELDS THAT PIONEERS PLANTED THAT AREN'T THERE ANYMORE!!! NEAR MARKER #2—LOOK TO THE LEFT AND RIGHT

SPECIAL HINT: You are standing in the middle of what was once a pioneer's cornfield! Whenever you see a group of tall skinny trees (tulip trees), you are very likely looking at what was once a farm field. Across from marker #2 there is a *very* tall tulip tree. Look up high to find the leaf that is shaped kind of like a tulip flower. Sometimes you need binoculars to see the leaves on these very tall trees! Mountain folks liked to use this tall straight tree for building cabins and barns. The tulip trees grew so big pioneers could build an entire cabin out of one tree!!!

_____10 points

#3 FIND THE FURRY VINE!!! NEAR MARKER #2

SPECIAL HINT: This poison ivy is climbing a tree and even though it looks like it is covered with fur, *do not pet it!* Why not?? You would itch like crazy! Poison ivy also grows on the ground and can be identified by its groupings of three leaves. Two good rhymes to remember are "Leaves of three! Let them be!" "Furry Vine! Itch in time!" Poison ivy's grape-like clusters of fruits are a favorite of many birds in the Smokies! Even though the fruit also contains the "poison," it doesn't bother the birds one bit! Lucky birds!!!

_____10 points

#4 FIND THE OLD ROAD THAT PIONEER KIDS USED TO WALK TO SCHOOL!!! AT MARKER #3—LOOK TOWARD THE CREEK

SPECIAL HINT: There are three roads at this spot in the trail.

Road #1—The actual creek bed was the first "road" that Indians and pioneers used. That was a very rough and wet road!

Road #2—The settlers cleared roads right _next_ to the creek.

Road #3—Then mountain folks built roads on higher levels to avoid flood situations. The trail you are hiking on is Road #3. *Can you find Road #2?*

Pioneer children walked on Road #2 all the way to <u>Fighting Creek School</u>, about a half-mile downstream! Pioneer families would also walk to church down this road! People lived in Forks of the River until 1935 when they had to leave because it was decided the Smoky Mountains would become a national park!

_____**10 points**

#5 FIND THE STRANGELY SHAPED ROCKING CHAIR TREE!!! JUST BEFORE YOU CROSS THE FOOTBRIDGE

SPECIAL HINT: Old-timers say a pioneer used the wood from this tree to build rocking chairs and as he kept pruning the tree branches to make the chairs, it grew in a very _wild and crazy_ way! Sycamore trees were also used by pioneers to make butcher blocks. By the way, this *is* a sycamore tree! You will now cross "Fighting Creek." Are you wondering how it got it's name? One reason is that the folks here fought a lot about where the community's school would be built. So they ended up calling the creek in the area "Fighting Creek" and the school was called "Fighting Creek School"!!!

_____**10 points**

#6 FIND THE DOG TRAP!!! 18 STEPS AFTER YOU CROSS THE FOOTBRIDGE—ON THE LEFT

SPECIAL HINT: Look for the evergreen plant that has sharp edges on its leathery leaves. It grows low to the ground and in the pioneer days dogs would get trapped or "hobbled" in the tangled growth. That's why this shrub was called dog-hobble by the pioneers! To really be sure you have found the dog-hobble, run your finger along the edge of a leaf. Does it feel sharp? Yes! You found the dog-hobble!!! *Remember! Protect every treasure in the Great Smoky Mountains National Park! Don't pick anything! Don't take anything! Don't leave anything!*

_____**10 points**

#7 FIND THE *WILD* WILD GRAPEVINES!!! 68 STEPS PAST THE
DOG-HOBBLE YOU JUST FOUND—LOOK AROUND

SPECIAL HINT: The woody vines are growing around the tree, up the tree, and down the tree! You can find lots of wild grapevines in the Smoky Mountains! Opossums and many other Smoky Mountain critters eat the sour wild grapes! Cherokee Indians would burn grapevines with oak because they believed it would bring a spell of warm weather in the middle of a cold winter. Cherokee Indians lived here long long ago and still live on the Qualla Indian Reservation on the other side of the mountains in Cherokee, North Carolina.

_____**10 points**

#8 FIND WHERE PIONEER NOAH McCARTER LIVED!!!
NEAR MARKER #5.

SPECIAL HINT: Find the dark-green round-shaped bush with tiny little oval leaves. This is a boxwood. Also find yucca plants that are low to the ground with leaves that are long, narrow, and pointed. The plants were used to landscape around the homestead. They are not native to the Smokies! Any time you see landscaping plants like these or yellow daffodils, a pioneer likely lived nearby.

_____**10 points**

#9 FIND THE FAMILY GARDEN!!! STAND AT THE BOXWOOD
BUSH AND FACE NORTH

SPECIAL HINT: Use the sun to find the direction and look across the trail. This pioneer family's garden was to the right of the cabin location. Settlers grew most of their own food. To feel like a pioneer, stop right where you are and pretend that you are going to build a cabin, farm this land, and provide for your family starting right here . . . today! You have a lot of hard work ahead of you! Early settlers had a tough row to hoe!!!

_____**10 points**

#10 FIND THE TREE IN THE MIDDLE OF THE TRAIL!!!
BETWEEN MARKER #5 AND MARKER #6

      SPECIAL HINT: You are searching for a maple tree growing smack-dab in the middle of the trail. Just don't run into it and bang your head!!!

            _____**10 points**

#11 FIND THE CHRISTMAS FERNS!!! GO 10 STEPS FROM THE
TREE THAT YOU JUST FOUND—LOOK ON THE RIGHT

      SPECIAL HINT: Some folks say that each individual fern leaf is shaped like Santa's sleigh and others say it is shaped like a Christmas stocking! Look to your right as you go up the hillside to find a Christmas fern. In the summer they may be hidden a bit, but as southerners might say, "Mayon—naise—a lot of 'em up there on the hill!" *Remember! Never pick anything, never take anything, and protect each and every plant and animal in this park!!!*

            _____**10 points**

#12 FIND THE TREE THAT ONCE BLOCKED THE TRAIL!!!
RIGHT BEFORE MARKER #7—NEAR THE TOP OF THE HILL

      SPECIAL HINT: The space between the rings in the trunk of the tree will be narrow for a very dry year and a bit wider for a very rainy year. Each ring is one-year's growth. If you are tired, lay on the bench, close your eyes, and count tree rings!!!

            _____**10 points**

#13 FIND THE LARGE ROCK WHERE AN "X" MARKS THE SPOT!!! IMMEDIATELY AFTER YOU CROSS THE NEXT FOOTBRIDGE

SPECIAL HINT: This rock has two cracks in it shaped very much like an "X." When water on a rock freezes, it expands in the little crevices and cracks the rock. That could be what happened to this one!

_____**10 points**

#14 FIND THE WOODEN PEGS ON THE CABIN!!! ON ONLY *ONE* OF THE OUTSIDE FOUR CORNERS OF JOHN OWNBY'S CABIN

SPECIAL HINT: Find the top of the wooden pegs used to hold the cabin together. Mysteriously, they are found *only* on one outside corner of this cabin!

_____**10 points**

#15 FIND JOHN OWNBY'S REFRIGERATOR!!! GO THROUGH THE CABIN AND HEAD TOWARD THE HILL—LOOK FOR THE STREAM AND A STACK OF ROCKS

SPECIAL HINT: John Ownby built a small shed around the spring and the flowing water kept his eggs and milk cool. A "springhouse" was a pioneer's refrigerator. How cool is that?

_____**10 points**

#16 FIND THE CORNFIELD A PIONEER COULD HAVE FALLEN OUT OF!!! AS YOU LEAVE THE SPRING TAKE 10 STEPS TOWARD THE CABIN

SPECIAL HINT: Look up to your left. Corn was actually grown on this steep hill. Mountain people joked about "falling out of their cornfields!" At harvest time pioneers used sleds to take the corn out of these steep fields!!!

_____**10 points**

#17 FIND SOMETHING YOU REALLY NEED BAD!!!
CROSS THE FOOTBRIDGE AND GO TO MARKER #10

SPECIAL HINT: This is a long hill! You may need a - - - - -! Some folks think Smoky Mountain benches are another Smoky Mountain *treasure* especially when they are tired and need a break!!!

_____**10 points**

#18 FIND THE "WINDOW" THROUGH THE OLD OAK TREE!!! FROM MARKER #10 TAKE ONE SHARP RIGHT TURN—THEN BEFORE THE NEXT SHARP RIGHT TURN— STOP AND LOOK

SPECIAL HINT: Before heading down the hill, look to the right of the path for a tree trunk that splits into a "Y" and creates a "window" down into the valley. There is a rock at the base of this tree that a shorter person may use as a footstool to peer through the "window" of this tree!!!

_____**10 points**

#19 FIND THE AMAZING WALL OF ROOTS!!! YOU'LL HIKE A WHILE—LOOK AT THE BOTTOM OF THE HILL—AS THE TRAIL BENDS TO THE LEFT

SPECIAL HINT: Two trees were blown over to create this incredible wall of roots! These trees will most likely become a home for many plants and animals in this forest! Check it out! Do you see any plants or Smoky Mountain critters that have decided to make it "home sweet home"? Don't forget to stop by the Sugarland's Visitor's Center and take a good look at all the critters that live in our National Park! You can also watch a great 20-minute movie all about the Smoky Mountains!

_____**10 points**

CONGRATULATIONS!!!

YOU HAVE JUST COMPLETED A
GREAT SMOKY MOUNTAINS NATIONAL PARK

SCAVENGER HIKE ADVENTURE!!!

<u>Fighting Creek Nature Trail</u>

TEN POINTS FOR EACH ITEM
FOUND
TOTAL SCORE _____

CERTIFIED ACHIEVEMENT
LEVEL_____

over 50 to 100 points:	**<u>City Slicker</u>**
over 100 to 170 points:	**<u>Pioneer Scout</u>**
over 170 points:	**<u>Frontier Explorer</u>**

Name(s): _____

_____

Witness(es) thereof: _____

Date: _____

GREAT SMOKY MOUNTAINS

Scavenger Hike Adventure #10

Smokemont Nature Trail

Why This Is a Great Trail! Camping in Smokemont near Cherokee, North Carolina??? This trail is just a short walk from your pup tent! Don't miss this pleasant mountain Scavenger Hike Adventure on the North Carolina side of the Smokies! This is a narrow, sometimes rather steep trail that is very do-able for families. The trail loops around a mountain ridge through a former logging area! You'll find three log footbridges that total over 100 feet long crossing over the beautiful mountain stream. You'll search for one of the most unusual chestnut tree hulks imaginable. It is HUGE!!! You'll hike through a rhododendron and mountain laurel "jungle." You will loop up, around, and back down the mountain. You'll definitely be comin' roun' the mountain when you come!!! Excellent for pioneers of all ages.

Where's the Trail? This trail is located 3 miles north of the Oconaluftee Visitor Center near the Cherokee, North Carolina, entrance to the park. From the Sugarlands Visitor Center, you should head straight over the mountains toward Cherokee on Newfound Gap Road (Rt. 441). Enter the Smokemont campground and drive to Section B, where there is parking at the trailhead.

About the Trail: Smokemont Nature Trail is rather narrow, sometimes a bit steep, but pretty easy.

<u>How Long Is This Hike?</u> This trail is about 3/4 of a mile loop and will take less than an hour.

<u>Things to Hunt For</u>
(Earn 10 points for each treasure you find)

#1 FIND THE TRIPLE FOOTBRIDGE!!! LOCATED AT THE TRAILHEAD—CROSS ONLY THE FIRST TWO BRIDGES AND THEN STOP AND FIND ITEM #2

SPECIAL HINT: You'll cross mountain streams on three footbridges that, in total, span over 100 feet! This is an awesome stream! It is beautiful Bradley Fork!!!

(Remember, don't cross the third log bridge until you complete #2)

_____10 points

#2 FIND THE "THERMOMETER" BUSHES!!! LOOK AROUND BETWEEN THE SECOND AND THIRD FOOTBRIDGE

SPECIAL HINT: Find the bush that has long narrow evergreen leaves that feel almost like leather. These are rhododendron bushes! The pioneers knew that at 32 degrees the leaves darken and droop, at 20 degrees they begin to curl up, and at 0 degrees the leaves curl up as tight as pencils! It is a "thermometer" in the woods! These rhododendron bushes bloom in the early summer!

_____10 points

#3 FIND THE "LANDING ZONE" FOR SMOKY MOUNTAIN NORTHERN FLYING SQUIRRELS!!! AFTER YOU CROSS THE THIRD LOG FOOTBRIDGE—GO 10 STEPS CURVING RIGHT ON A SMALL PATH LEADING DOWN TO THE STREAM

SPECIAL HINT: Look at the boulder next to the stream. Do you see something that looks like brownish colored crumpled leaves growing on the rocks? This is rock tripe, a favorite snack of northern flying squirrels!!! It is a lichen (pronounced "like-in") and is a combination of fungus and algae. This rock tripe releases an acid that eats away at the rock. This acid will eventually break this rock into fine particles that will then turn into soil. Pretty amazing, huh??? Don't eat the rock tripe unless you are a flying squirrel! Northern flying squirrels are generally found in higher elevations in the park so they may find a different landing zone to enjoy this snack!

_____**10 points**

#4 FIND THE SPOON, I MEAN "FORK" IN THE RIVER!!! AS YOU HIKE UP THE RIDGE OF THE MOUNTAIN—LOOK DOWN AT THE STREAM

SPECIAL HINT: Find where the beautiful stream splits like a kitchen fork with two prongs!

_____**10 points**

#5 FIND THE LOGGING VILLAGE DOWN BELOW!!! AT MARKER #2— LOOK DOWN INTO THE VALLEY—ON THE RIGHT

SPECIAL HINT: It is hard to believe that this campground area below you once had homes, a store, a railroad, and was a bustling logging community! Before this area was a park, a logging company cut down most of the trees including those on the mountain you are now climbing! That is why the forest all around you is called a "second growth forest!"

_____**10 points**

#6 FIND THE BENCH AND TAKE A "SMELL" BREAK!!! NEAR MARKER #4

SPECIAL HINT: The evergreen tree behind the log has short flat needles with two white stripes on the underneath side of each needle. If you gently rub the needles between your fingers it gives off a great smell! Take a smell break! This tree is a hemlock. *Now* you know how to identify one of the more than 130 different kinds (species) of trees in the Great Smoky Mountains National Park!!!

_____**10 points**

#7 FIND THE HILL OF ROOTS!!!
LOCATED NEAR MARKER #6

SPECIAL HINT: Look up the hill on the right side of the trail. These tree roots have to find food and water! They are searching everywhere! Can you match a root with its tree? The Smoky Mountains is a very rocky place. There are lots of rocks and sometimes erosion causes there to be very little soil on the trail! It's truly amazing how tree roots will sometimes even break right through rocks in the Smokies looking for food and water!

_____**10 points**

#8 FIND THE MOUNTAIN LAUREL JUNGLE!!! 45 STEPS PAST MARKER #6

SPECIAL HINT: You are surrounded by mountain laurel! Mountain laurel looks a lot like rhododendron but has narrower and shorter evergreen leaves. Mountain laurel has beautiful white and pink flowers that bloom in the spring and in the summer in higher elevations. Pioneers called it "ivy." Cherokee Indians who lived in the Smokies long long ago and still live in Cherokee, North Carolina today called mountain laurel "spoonwood" because they carved spoons from it! If you're lucky— you'll be hiking in a beautiful bouquet of flowers!!!

_____**10 points**

#9 FIND THE TREE THAT BLEW OVER AND LANDED ON THE TRAIL!!! GO 20 STEPS PAST MARKER #8

SPECIAL HINT: Park rangers had to cut this tree with a chain saw to make an opening for you to get through! Special thanks to our park rangers who help take care of this beautiful park!!! *It is up to all of us to protect every single treasure in the Smoky Mountains! Remember! Don't take anything! Don't pick anything! And don't leave anything!*

_____10 points

#10 FIND A CHRISTMAS FERN!!!
AT MARKER #10

SPECIAL HINT: Some folks think that the individual leaves of this fern are shaped like Santa's sleigh or a Christmas stocking and that is why it was named Christmas Fern! What do you think??? There are many very beautiful ferns in the Smoky Mountains!

_____10 points

#11 FIND THE GRAY GHOST!!! 24 STEPS PAST MARKER #11

SPECIAL HINT: Look up the hill—on the left. This is the remains of a giant chestnut tree. Wow!!! In the early 1900s these trees were wiped out by a blight (disease). The mountain folks thought the huge gray stumps looked like gray ghosts in the evening mist. It was said that cabins built from a chestnut tree would never rot! Bears loved the chestnuts and so did people! Bears are smaller today than they were when they had chestnuts to eat!

_____10 points

100

SPECIAL COMMENTS: Visit the campground office and check out the display of old photographs taken during the logging days! Smokemont sure didn't look like a campground back then!

On your way out of the campground, park right before the bridge and walk up the hill to the Lufty Baptist Church established in 1836. Go inside and take a look at where early settlers worshipped!

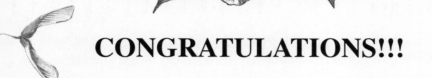

CONGRATULATIONS!!!

YOU HAVE JUST COMPLETED A
GREAT SMOKY MOUNTAINS NATIONAL PARK

SCAVENGER HIKE ADVENTURE!!!

<u>Smokemont Nature Trail</u>

TEN POINTS FOR EACH ITEM FOUND

TOTAL SCORE _____

CERTIFIED ACHIEVEMENT

LEVEL_____

over 50 to 70 points: <u>**City Slicker**</u>

over 70 to 90 points: <u>**Pioneer Scout**</u>

over 90 points: <u>**Frontier Explorer**</u>

Name(s): _____

_____

Witness(es) thereof: _____

Date: _____

GREAT SMOKY MOUNTAINS

Scavenger Hike Adventure #11

Grapeyard Ridge Trail
to Steam Engine Wreck (EXTREME)

Why This Is a Great Trail! This Scavenger Hike Adventure will lead you through Rhododendron Valley, one of the most peaceful and beautiful narrow low-land valleys imaginable! You will find the area where Dolly Parton's grandfather, Walter Parton, once lived. You will cross streams a challenging half-dozen times. There are no footbridges and one stream is almost 10 feet wide!!! You won't believe it when you find a steam engine that rolled off the side of the mountain and landed in Injun Creek! Depending on the time of year, you might not even see one other hiker on this beautiful trail in the quieter and less busy Greenbrier section of the park!

Where's the Trail? From the Sugarlands Visitor Center go north on Rt. 441 into Gatlinburg. Be sure to merge into the right lane when you see the Hard Rock Café and then veer right onto US 321 at **stoplight #3.** Stoplights in Gatlinburg are all numbered. Follow US 321 approximately 6 miles to the Greenbrier entrance of the Great Smoky Mountains National Park. Turn right into the park and drive along the Little Pigeon River on Greenbrier Road for about 3 miles until you see the bridge and road that leads to Ramsey Cascades Trail. Park on the left side of Greenbrier road before the bridge. The trailhead is on the right side of the road.

About the Trail: The trail climbs a ridge before it heads down into Rhododendron Valley. After about 2 miles, the trail heads uphill for 7/10 of a mile to the top of James Gap. Then it heads downhill for 2/10 of a mile to the steam engine wreck lying in Injun Creek. It is a fairly solid uphill trek to the top of James Gap.

How Long Is This Hike? This Scavenger Hike Adventure is a little over 6 miles roundtrip. It is do-able in 3–4 hours.

Things to Hunt For
(Earn 10 points for each treasure you find)

#1 FIND THE ANSWERS TO TWO SMOKY MOUNTAIN FISHING QUESTIONS!!! ACROSS THE ROAD FROM THE TRAILHEAD

SPECIAL HINT: Answer true or false.
#1 It is a good idea to use worms and corn for bait when fishing in the park. (T or F)
#2 The maximum number of fish you can keep is two per day. (T or F)

_____10 points

#2 FIND THE PICTURE WINDOW!!! JUST AS YOU START UP THE TRAIL—LOOK TO THE LEFT

SPECIAL HINT: Look for two trees bordering a large rock. The trees and the rock form a perfect "picture window" overlooking a beautiful view of the cascading creek across Greenbrier Road! Two creeks, the Middle Prong of the Little Pigeon River and Porter's Creek come tumbling out of the mountains and join together here to become the Little Pigeon River! *Warning: Don't touch the furry vine growing around the "frame" of the picture window—POISON IVY!!!*

_____10 points

#3 FIND THE ROCK WALL BUILT BY THE YOUNG MEN OF THE CCC!!! AS YOU CONTINUE A FEW STEPS UP THE RIDGE—LOOK TO THE RIGHT

SPECIAL HINT: The Civilian Conservation Corps had a camp just south of the trailhead on Greenbrier Road. The CCC was a program started by the U.S. government in the 1930s to give jobs to young men during the depression when few jobs were available. Those young men of the CCC built this rock wall and built this *entire trail*. We can thank the CCC for many of the trails and bridges in the park! If you need to mail something or get some groceries, there is a grocery store and post office right above the rock wall. Oh sorry, I guess that was about 80 years ago! The only thing left now is a piece of a chimney.

_____**10 points**

#4 FIND THE WOOD THAT THE CHEROKEE INDIANS BELIEVED WOULD CHANGE THE WEATHER!!! BETWEEN HERE AND THE STEAM ENGINE WRECK

SPECIAL HINT: Find a wild grapevine! Cherokee Indians have lived in the Smokies for about 1,000 years. They believed that burning the wood of a grapevine with oak would bring a warm spell of weather in the middle of a cold winter. If it looks like a grapevine but has a furry cover—you probably found poison ivy! Keep looking!!! This entire area was once called **Winnesoka,** Cherokee for "Place of the Grapes." White settlers did not use that name, but did use the name "grapeyard" for the high ridge extending above Round Top Mountain. When this trail was built it was also named Grapeyard Ridge linking back to the original Cherokee name *Winnesoka!*

_____**10 points**

#5 FIND A SPECIAL PLANT THAT IS ONLY FOUND IN THE APPALACHIAN MOUNTAINS!!! SEARCH ALL ALONG THE TRAIL UP THIS RIDGE

SPECIAL HINT: Find galax (pronounced "gay-lax"), a plant with very shiny green leaves shaped like fat hearts. It only grows a few inches off the ground. In the spring it blooms a white pillar of flowers that smells like garlic. The mountain folks would sell the galax leaves to florists for use in floral arrangements. In the fall, galax turns crimson red. If you can't find them here, you can always search in Galax, Virginia! *Remember! Don't pick anything. All plants are protected by our national park. Picking a plant or flower can bring a stiff fine from the federal government.*

_____**10 points**

#6 FIND THE REMAINS OF A SETTLER'S HOMESITE!!! HIKE ABOUT 10–15 MINUTES—LOOK ON THE RIGHT AT <u>EYE LEVEL</u>—AT THE TOP OF THE HILL WHERE THE TRAIL SHARPLY BENDS TO THE RIGHT AND STARTS HEADING DOWN

SPECIAL HINT: Look for the mound of rocks that was once the chimney and fireplace about 30 feet to the right of the trail. This pioneer had a choice *corner* lot on top of this beautiful ridge! <u>Remember: It is about a 15-minute hike from the start of the trail to the top of this first hill.</u> There is a very large curving bend to the right as it heads down into Rhododendron Valley.

_____**10 points**

#7 FIND A STAND OF HEMLOCK TREES!!! ON THE LEFT—AS YOU HEAD DOWN THE HILL FROM THE SETTLER'S HOMESITE

SPECIAL HINT: A grouping of the same kind of tree is called a "stand." Find the stand of hemlocks. A hemlock needle is about as long as a fingernail and has two faint white stripes on the underside. Hemlocks in the park are being attacked by an insect called the hemlock wooly adelgid (a-dell-jid). Hemlocks cool the mountain streams and if they die, the water temperature will rise and then threaten fish and other animals. Seven species of songbirds depend on hemlocks for food and shelter. In nature it seems everything is connected. Rangers are doing everything they can to save these important trees.

_____**10 points**

#8 FIND A SIGN OF A BEAR!!! LOOK ALL ALONG THE TRAIL FROM HERE TO THE WRECKED ENGINE—GO ON TO #9 AS YOU KEEP YOUR EYES WIDE OPEN

SPECIAL HINT: This is a fairly secluded trail and there are about two bears for every square mile in the park! Remember you drove over 3 miles deep into the woods on Greenbrier Road before you even started this hike!!! Look for a tree or log that was clawed open by a bear searching for insects to eat. Bears also eat berries and yellow jackets!!! Look for black bear scat—which is often a shiny blackish-blueish when berries are in season. There is a lot of bear activity on this trail! Keep your eyes wide open!!! If you can't find any sign of a bear, but _actually find a bear_ along the trail—_go ahead and give yourself the points anyway!!!_

_____**10 points**

#9 FIND THE SITE OF AVERY WHALEY'S FARM AND ORCHARD!!! AFTER YOU CROSS THE FIRST STREAM LOOK ON THE LEFT AND RIGHT OF THE TRAIL FOR FLAT OPEN AREAS

SPECIAL HINT: The skinny trees and open spaces around you are a clue that this was once a cleared farm field. Avery Whaley had about 50 apple trees in his orchard and he also farmed this area. Many families once lived along the rich "bottom land" near the creek in this beautiful valley! You may notice the "zillions" of delicate lady ferns all along the trail!

_____10 points

#10 FIND THE AREA ONCE HOME TO DOLLY PARTON'S GRANDFATHER, WALTER PARTON!!! JUST BEFORE YOU CROSS THE SECOND STREAM FIND THE REMAINS OF A ROCK WALL ON THE LEFT

SPECIAL HINT: This area certainly wasn't Dolly's Woods, but it was Walter's Woods! Many of Dolly's kinfolk lived in what is now the national park. Walter Parton lived up above the creek in this area on the left. He definitely didn't work just 9 to 5!!!

_____10 points

#11 FIND THE QUARTZ BOULDERS!!! 40 STEPS PAST THE SECOND STREAM CROSSING

SPECIAL HINT: Look for a whitish-brownish-orange boulder the size of a wheelbarrow! It should be easy to spot. There are a few of them along the trail here.

_____10 points

#12 FIND RHODODENDRON VALLEY!!! ALL AROUND YOU AS YOU CONTINUE PAST THE QUARTZ BOULDERS

SPECIAL HINT: The rhododendron bush has long narrow evergreen leaves that feel almost like leather. Mountain folks used to call rhododendron "laurel" so this valley was originally called Laurel Valley. When the park was formed there were too many Laurel Creeks and Laurel Valleys so they changed the name of the creek and the valley to "Rhododendron." There are also many mountain laurel bushes in this valley. They look similar to rhododendron bushes except the leaves are smaller. When mountain laurel or rhododendron is in bloom, you may feel like you are walking through a postcard!!!

_____**10 points**

#13 FIND THE LOG ACROSS THE CREEK THAT COULD LEAD YOU IN THE WRONG DIRECTION!!! AT THE NEXT STREAM CROSSING

SPECIAL HINT: You'll come to a very wide stream crossing. There is a tree that fell across the stream on the left and it is a tempting bridge! ***Caution: This log points away from the actual trail and is a hazardous route!*** The trail picks up a bit upstream from the crossing point (to your right). Your best bet is to use the rocks as stepping stones or *give it up* and just wade through the shallow stream. <u>Veer to the right immediately after you cross the stream</u> to get back on the trail!

_____**10 points**

#14 FIND THE FENCE POSTS!!! CROSS THREE MORE STREAMS—SEARCH ON THE RIGHT SIDE OF THE TRAIL

SPECIAL HINT: Some of the fence posts still have barbed-wire attached! If you are really observant you can determine the entire area that this settler fenced in. Another clue is to carefully look about 20 steps before you reach a small low-lying water crossing. Good luck. This one is kind of tough!!!

_____**10 points**

#15 FIND SIGNS OF WILD HOGS!!! ALONG THE TRAIL—BETWEEN HERE AND THE STEAM ENGINE WRECK—GO ON TO #16 WHILE YOU SEARCH

SPECIAL HINT: Look for areas on the ground and even on the side of the trail where wild hogs used their snouts and rooted the ground to find food. The wild hogs eat about anything on the ground including snails, snakes, acorns, roots, flowers, and salamanders. Some park rangers are employed full-time to hunt for hogs because they are not native to the park and they destroy plant life and pollute the streams. Hundreds still roam the park at night!

_____**10 points**

#16 FIND THE CABIN LOCATION AT THE ABSOLUTE TOP OF JAMES GAP!!! AFTER YOU *FINALLY* MAKE IT TO THE TOP OF THE RIDGE (<u>ABOUT 7/10 MILE UPHILL HIKE</u>) FIND THE MOUND OF ROCKS ABOVE YOU ON THE RIGHT—MARKING THE FIREPLACE AND LOCATION OF THE CABIN

SPECIAL HINT: It is a long challenging hike up to this gap! You may wonder if you will ever make it. You did!!! The steam engine wreck is only 2/10 of a mile down from here. Remember, the return hike is mainly downhill!

_____**10 points**

#17 FIND THE STEAM ENGINE WRECK!!!

HEAD DOWN THE HILL—LOOK IN THE CREEK

SPECIAL HINT: This old steam engine was self-propelled and was used for logging. It rolled off the mountain over 80 years ago. Its been said that the engineer jumped to safety and did not get hurt. The steam engine was being used to help build a school.

_____**10 points**

#18 FIND THE NAME OF THE COMPANY THAT MANUFACTURED THIS STEAM ENGINE!!!

LOCATED ON THE ENGINE

SPECIAL HINT: Head down toward the engine! This is a very unique historical treasure of the Smokies!!!

_____**10 points**

CONGRATULATIONS!!!

YOU HAVE JUST COMPLETED A
GREAT SMOKY MOUNTAINS NATIONAL PARK

SCAVENGER HIKE ADVENTURE!!!

<u>Grapeyard Ridge Trail to</u>
<u>Steam Engine Wreck (EXTREME)</u>

TEN POINTS FOR EACH ITEM FOUND

TOTAL SCORE _____

CERTIFIED ACHIEVEMENT

LEVEL_____

over 50 to 100 points: <u>City Slicker</u>
over 100 to 150 points: <u>Pioneer Scout</u>
over 150 points: <u>Frontier Explorer</u>

Name(s): _____

_____

Witness(es) thereof: _____

Date: _____

GREAT SMOKY MOUNTAINS

Scavenger Hike Adventure #12

<u>Cosby Nature Trail</u>

<u>Why This Is a Great Trail!</u> This Scavenger Hike Adventure is on a trail that is a hidden jewel in the Smokies! You will enjoy the "surround sounds" of water as you cross streams <u>eight</u> times on log bridges! This trail has many huge hemlock trees and it is <u>always</u> damp and shaded by the lush green forest. On a hot day, this cool trail is the ticket!! You'll search for a tree that was ripped apart by a bear, a family's garden from long ago, a tree that looks like an elbow, and a trunk of a tree you can stand in! This trail is on the "quiet" side of the park near Cosby, and it is worth every single minute of the drive over!!! There is also a picnic area near the trailhead. You might want to pack some PB&Js!

<u>Where's the Trail?</u> From the Sugarlands Visitor Center go north on Rt. 441 into Gatlinburg. Veer right onto US 321 right past the Hard Rock Café at **stoplight #3** (stoplights in Gatlinburg are all numbered with big signs). Follow US 321 until you can't go any farther. At that "T" in the road turn right (south) toward Cosby Campground and in about 1 mile you'll see the Cosby park entrance on the right. Drive *past* the picnic area and campground reservation office and you'll see the sign for the Cosby Nature Trail. There is a small parking area near the amphitheater.

About the Trail: This hike is a level walk with a nicely cleared trail of gravel, stones, and forest mulch. There are many great places to sit by the water and cool off. This trail reminds us of the forest scene in the movie *Wizard of Oz,* except there are no tigers. This is one of our favorite nature trails in the entire park! Don't miss it!!!

How Long Is This Hike? This Scavenger Hike Adventure is less than a mile roundtrip and will take about an hour or less to complete.

A Brief Comment About the Cosby Side of the Park: This part of the Great Smoky Mountains National Park gets very minimal use because it is not close to go-cart tracks or fudge shops. It is quiet, has practically no traffic, and is an easy and scenic country drive to get there! It is a beautiful part of the park with trails that lead to vista views and a waterfall!

Things to Hunt For
(Earn 10 points for each treasure you find)

#1 FIND THE HOMESITE OF A FAMILY WHO LIVED HERE LONG LONG AGO!!!
LEFT OF THE PARKING LOT AND JUST LEFT OF THE NATURE TRAILHEAD SIGN

SPECIAL HINT: Before you enter the trail, look for the stack of rocks that was once a fireplace! Families lived throughout this area even back in the 1800s. There once was a huge apple orchard nearby! Fireplace and chimney remains (such as this one) or even yellow daffodils often mark the spot of a former homesite.

_____**10 points**

#2 FIND THE OLD WAGON ROAD!!!

AFTER YOU GO DOWN THE LITTLE HILL AND GET
ON THE TRAIL

SPECIAL HINT: Look down the trail to your right and then to your left! Where you are now standing used to be the wagon road for the community that existed here. Amazing, isn't it? The road ran right by the old homesite you just discovered!

_____**10 points**

#3 FIND THE MOUNTAIN SPRING!!! AS SOON AS YOU GET ON THE TRAIL LOOK DOWN THE SIDE OF THE HILL TOWARD THE STREAM

SPECIAL HINT: Look for a white pipe sticking out of the side of the hill! The water from this spring was called "free stone water" by the local mountain people because it had few minerals in it. In other words, the water tasted sweet compared to some spring water that contained a lot of iron or other not so tasty minerals. *You should <u>never</u> drink any water in the park's streams or springs without treating it by boiling or purifying it with chemicals.*

_____**10 points**

#4 SMELL A HEMLOCK!!!

ON THE LEFT SIDE OF THE TRAIL—FIND AN EVERGREEN TREE
WITH SHORT FLAT NEEDLES ABOUT AS LONG AS YOUR FINGERNAIL.

SPECIAL HINT: Check on the underside of a branch. If each needle has two white stripes—you've found a hemlock! Gently rub the needles of the tree between your thumb and fingers and then take a whiff. Now, the next time someone asks if you have ever really smelled a hemlock tree say, **"Uh"** (Cherokee for "yes") and then say, **"Zee-yookt guh-noh-hee-ahay"** (Cherokee for "I speak the truth"). Indians lived in these parts for thousands of years. Many Cherokee Indians still live on the Qualla Indian Reservation on the other side of this mountain range in Cherokee, North Carolina!

_____**10 points**

#5 FIND THE TREE WITH AN "ELBOW"!!! ON THE RIGHT OF THE TRAIL AS YOU PASS THE AMPHITHEATER ABOVE YOU

SPECIAL HINT: This tree is located <u>before</u> you get to the first stream crossing and is very unusual because the trunk has grown in a curve that looks like a giant arm and elbow!!!

_____10 points

#6 FIND THE "HORNED" TREE!!! ON THE LEFT SIDE OF THE TRAIL AT THE FIRST STREAM CROSSING

SPECIAL HINT: Stand at the edge of the shallow stream and look to your left. In shaded forests, such as this one, hemlock trees put all their energy "to grow" at the top searching for the sun and that is why lower branches rot away and create these dead branches that look like "horns." The branches at the top of this tree have found the sun and they are doing great!!!

_____10 points

#7 FIND THE WILD GRAPEVINE!!! STAND ON THE LOG FOOTBRIDGE—LOOK TO THE LEFT

SPECIAL HINT: Look up! This long woody wild grapevine is growing very high in a tree! Opossums and skunks and many other Smoky Mountain critters snack on the wild grapes!!!

_____10 points

#8 FIND THE TREE THAT WAS CLAWED BY A BLACK BEAR!!! GO TO THE <u>NEXT</u> FOOTBRIDGE—COUNT 50 STEPS PAST THE BRIDGE—THEN SEARCH ON THE RIGHT SIDE OF THE TRAIL

SPECIAL HINT: Bears will often tear into trees searching for honey, grubs, termites, and other small squiggly snacks. What are you having for lunch? There are about 2,000 bears in the park and that means there are about two bears for every square mile. Bears are often high up in the treetops. They are great climbers! Quick!!! Look up!!!

_____**10 points**

#9 FIND THE DOG-HOBBLE!!! AT MARKER #3

SPECIAL HINT: Look for a low bush with sharp-edged leaves. Do the test and gently rub your finger back and forth across the edges to see if they are sharp. Long ago settlers' dogs would chase after bears and would get stuck in these bushes. They sure could make a dog "hobble." The bears would run right through. So now you know why it is called dog-hobble! While you are at this spot, check out the "eagle claw" at the top of a tree!!!

_____**10 points**

#10 FIND THE "SPIDER" TREE!!! NEAR MARKER #4

SPECIAL HINT: New trees will sometimes grow out of a dead tree trunk. The roots of the *new* tree will grow around the trunk of the *dead* tree. Years later the dead trunk rots away and leaves roots that are standing up off the ground and sort of look like legs of a spider!

_____**10 points**

#11 FIND THE "WIZARD OF OZ" JUNGLE!!! AFTER THE NEXT TWO LOG FOOTBRIDGES—AS YOU HEAD UP A SLOPE

SPECIAL HINT: Trust me! As you hike up the slope, you'll *know* when you make it to the jungle, but don't expect to find a yellow brick road! The leaves of rhododendron are about as long as from the top of your head to your chin and are thick and leathery. You are in a jungle of them. Cherokee Indians, who lived here, carved pipes and toys using wood from this bush. They also placed a leaf on the forehead to cure a headache! *Remember! Never pick or take anything from this national park! Protect every treasure you see!*

_____**10 points**

#12 FIND THE FALLEN TREE THAT "BELONGS" TO THE STUMP!!! AT MARKER #6

SPECIAL HINT: There is a stump on the left of the path. Search for the tree that originally was connected to that stump! The stump and the fallen tree have both become homes for moss, ferns, and other plants and is also home for insects and possibly other Smoky Mountain critters.

_____**10 points**

#13 FIND THE SPICE BUSHES THE MOUNTAIN FOLKS USED TO MAKE TEA!!! ON THE RIGHT SIDE OF THE TRAIL AT MARKER #8

SPECIAL HINT: A large stack of stones marks the location of a fireplace and the site where someone lived long, long ago. Spice bushes are all around the fireplace. They are about as tall or a little taller than a person and have thin branches. Gently rub one of the branches with your fingernail and take a whiff! Mountain folks would break up the twigs of these bushes, boil them in water, and brew up some spicy lemony tea! It was also excellent seasoning for a delicious groundhog or opossom entree. Now—stay put at marker #8. *Remember . . . all plants are protected. Never pick or take anything from the park.*

_____**10 points**

#14 FIND THE LOCATION OF A FAMILY GARDEN FROM LONG LONG AGO!!! NEAR MARKER #8—ON THE LEFT SIDE OF THE TRAIL

SPECIAL HINT: Stone walls were built one heavy stone at a time! It was hard work building these walls! Often stones had to be cleared off the land to plant a garden because the Smoky Mountains is a *very* rocky place. Three walls still encircle what was once a family's vegetable garden. On the right side of the trail is their home-site. Speak a little Cherokee just for fun! Say to one of your fellow hikers **"Zah-we-shah-ohsh?"** That's Cherokee for "Do you have a garden?" Your fellow hiker can answer **"Uh"** which means "yes" or **"Hah-dee-yoh-gah"** which means "no."

_____**10 points**

#15 FIND THE CORNER OF ANOTHER OLD ROCK WALL!!! 50 STEPS PAST MARKER #8

SPECIAL HINT: This 90-degree rock wall corner is a good place to peer into the woods and imagine where the old pasture or field once was! You are standing in the middle of what was once farm fields and pastures! Young trees are now growing back. Imagine kids playing, gardens growing, and cows mooing! Okay, time to *"moooove"* on down the trail!!!

_____**10 points**

#16 FIND THE MOUNTAIN FAMILY'S SOURCE OF DRINKING WATER!!! AT MARKER #9

SPECIAL HINT: This mountain spring once had a small shed built around it (they called it a spring house) and settlers would store milk, eggs, and some meats around the flowing water. This was their refrigerator and their drinking fountain! Notice the rocks that the mountain folks put in this hole to keep the spring opened up. Pretty cool!

_____**10 points**

#17 FIND THE "APARTMENT HOUSE TREE" AND THE GRAPEVINES GONE WILD!!! JUST PAST MARKER #10—ON THE LEFT OF THE TRAIL

SPECIAL HINT: The bottom of this tree trunk looks as if it has small compartments or maybe "apartments"! Trees provide homes for many creatures in the forest. Smoky Mountain critters may find a place to sleep in these holes. Look around! Find the huge woody grapevines that have gone absolutely wild! Tarzan would really like this spot!!!

_____10 points

#18 FIND A VIRGINIA CREEPER CREEPING UP A TREE!!! 22 STEPS PAST MARKER #10—SEARCH ON THE LEFT

SPECIAL HINT: It looks sort of like a furry poison ivy vine, but has gnarly worm-like tentacles growing around its outside. Another clue is that it has five leaf groupings unlike poison ivy, which has "leaves of three." This creeper is non-poisonous.

_____10 points

#19 FIND A TREE GROWING OUT OF A HUMONGOUS <u>STUMP</u> OF ANOTHER TREE!!! ON THE RIGHT—AFTER A BACKWARD "S" CURVE IN THE TRAIL—LOOK ABOUT 15 FEET INTO THE WOODS

SPECIAL HINT: Dead tree trunks often are a very nourishing spot for a new tree to grow. Moisture, like you find on this trail, helps to make the environment perfect for dead logs to become new homes for other plants. Sometimes such a dead tree trunk is called a "nurse tree" because it is feeding and nourishing new plants and trees!

_____**10 points**

#20 STAND INSIDE THE TRUNK OF A TREE!!! ON THE LEFT— JUST BEFORE YOU REACH THE LOG FOOTBRIDGE

SPECIAL HINT: _Always check for Smoky Mountain critters before entering a tree trunk!_ Bears will often take a nap inside the hollow of a tree, therefore, to get the points it is recommended that you only _stand_ inside the tree trunk. Do not take a nap in there!!!

_____**10 points**

CONGRATULATIONS!!!

YOU HAVE JUST COMPLETED A
GREAT SMOKY MOUNTAINS NATIONAL PARK

SCAVENGER HIKE ADVENTURE!!!

<u>Cosby Nature Trail</u>

TEN POINTS FOR EACH ITEM FOUND

TOTAL SCORE _____

CERTIFIED ACHIEVEMENT

LEVEL_____

over 50 to 100 points: <u>City Slicker</u>
over 100 to 170 points: <u>Pioneer Scout</u>
over 170 points: <u>Frontier Explorer</u>

Name(s): _____

_____

Witness(es) thereof: _____

Date: _____

GREAT SMOKY MOUNTAINS

Scavenger Hike Adventures #13 and #14

<u>Alum Cave Bluffs Trail</u> <u>(MODERATELY EXTREME)</u> <u>and</u> <u>(EXTREMELY EXTREME</u> <u>OPTION): On Up to Mount</u> <u>LeConte</u>

<u>**Why This Is a Great Trail!**</u> Alum Cave Bluffs Trail is a humdinger of a hike!!! Many hikers rave that it is the most scenic hike in the Great Smoky Mountains National Park!!! On this Scavenger Hike Adventure you will follow Alum Cave Creek as you hike across many footbridges! Find *giant* hemlock trees that are hundreds of years old! Find signs of the tremendous flash flood that hit Mt. LeConte on Labor Day weekend in 1951! Hike <u>through</u> the inside of a giant rock formation called Arch Rock! You'll find cable "handrails" to assist you in steep areas with sheer drop-offs

and unbelievably incredible views!!! Find the needle hole in the side of a mountain, and be inspired at Inspiration Point! You'll find Alum Cave Bluffs! Whoa!!! It's unlike anything else you will ever see in the Great Smoky Mountains!!!

You may choose the *Extremely Extreme* option and continue on from the Bluffs another strenuous 2.8 miles to Mt. LeConte (elevation 6,593 feet). Mt. LeConte is over <u>a mile high</u> from its base!!! Along the way to Mt. LeConte you will find views that will *definitely*—and we mean <u>*definitely*</u>—knock your hiking socks off!!! You will find the most popular rustic lodge in the east that can only be reached on foot! Sit a spell in a rocking chair! You deserve it! Check out the panoramic views from Cliff Top!!!

<u>**Where's the Trail?**</u> From Sugarland's Visitor Center follow the signs toward Cherokee and Newfound Gap on highway Rt. 441 (Newfound Gap Road). At about 8.6 miles you will see a sign for Alum Cave Bluffs Trail. The trailhead and parking are on the left.

<u>**About the Trail:**</u> I'm not bluffin'! You may be huffin'! All the way to Arch Rock (1.3 miles) the trail is wide and fairly level. The trail then becomes much steeper as you continue on to Alum Cave Bluffs (about 2.2 miles from the trailhead). The cable handrail helps! At times the trail is rocky and narrow. This is absolutely—no doubt about it—worth tackling!

Going on to Mt. LeConte is strenuous and steep, but it is the most traveled route to the tippety top! Key tip: "Allow *plenty* of time and *take* your time."

<u>**How Long Is This Hike?**</u> This Scavenger Hike Adventure to Alum Cave Bluffs is 4.4 miles roundtrip and you should allow 3–4 hours.

Going on up to Mt. LeConte and searching around the top is about 10.5 miles roundtrip and you should allow 6–8 hours or more. You should plan this hike as a full-day trip! Definitely take plenty of water and plenty of food to keep up your energy on this *Extremely Extreme* Scavenger Hike Adventure! You can get more drinking water at the top for your trek down.

Things to Hunt For
(Earn 10 points for each treasure you find)

#1 FIND HOW *LONG* A TROUT MUST BE TO HAVE OVER TO YOUR HOUSE FOR DINNER!!! LOOK FOR THE SIGN AT THE TRAILHEAD

SPECIAL HINT: There are over 2,000 miles of streams in the Great Smoky Mountains!!! That's a lot of water and a lot of fish!!! Some streams in the Smokies have 2,000 to 4,000 trout per mile! If you catch a trout and take it home for dinner it better be at least ____ inches long! The national park protects the fish in these waters. As long as you follow the rules in the park, you can grab a pole and "Go Fish!!!"

_____10 points

#2 FIND THE OUTDOOR THERMOMETERS!!! AFTER YOU CROSS THE FOOTBRIDGE LOOK ON BOTH SIDES OF THE TRAIL

SPECIAL HINT: Do you notice any bushes with long, narrow, and thick dark green leaves? Look really hard . . . Not!!! You are totally surrounded!!! These rhododendron leaves stay green all year and will bloom with beautiful flowers in late spring and summer! The leaves will tell you the temperature! At 32 degrees they begin to darken and droop, at 20 degrees they roll up, and at 0 degrees they roll up as tight as a pencil! How cool is that! Pioneers actually used these plants as thermometers!!!

_____10 points

#3 FIND THE HUMONGOUS OLD HEMLOCK TREE!!! COUNT 60 STEPS FROM THE SECOND FOOTBRIDGE—LOOK *ACROSS* ALUM CAVE CREEK

SPECIAL HINT: Stand on a rock for the best view! This trail is home to some of the biggest and oldest trees in the park! Some hemlocks in the Smokies are 300–400 years old!!! This is an old growth northern hardwood and hemlock forest. This area of the park has never been logged and so it looks much like it did in the days of pioneers and Indians! That's why it's called an "old growth" forest. The beautiful hemlock trees in our park are being threatened by a tiny insect from Asia called the hemlock wooly adelgid (a-dell-jid). Our park rangers are doing everything they can to save these trees!

_____**10 points**

#4 FIND THE <u>GIANT</u> "HOLEY" HEMLOCK!!! ON THE RIGHT— IT IS PRACTICALLY <u>ON</u> THE TRAIL

SPECIAL HINT: Take a peck—I mean a peek! Woodpeckers have had a field day on this tree pecking holes as they looked for insects! You'll find a smaller holey hemlock before you reach this giant. Trust us! You'll know when you arrive at this tree! This tree is about 20 hiking boots (lady's size 8) around! Three people arm to arm may still not make it around the trunk! The tree has thick reddish-brown bark and lacy-looking branches of needles. This trail is famous for its giant hemlock trees and yellow birches!!!

_____**10 points**

#5 FIND THE BEAR HOBBLE . . . NOT!!!

40 STEPS PAST THE HOLEY TREE— LOOK ON BOTH SIDES OF THE TRAIL

SPECIAL HINT: This evergreen plant <u>would not</u> hobble a bear! Pioneer dogs, though, would get stuck or "hobbled" in these bushes as they tried to run through them to chase bears! The bears could run right through the bushes. That is why it is not called "bear hobble!" Feel the sharp edges of the leaves to make sure you've found it! Oh, by the way, it *is* called dog-hobble!

_____**10 points**

#6 FIND THE GIANT TREE ROOTS TRAVELING ACROSS THE TRAIL SEARCHING FOR FOOD!!! COUNT 50 STEPS PAST

THE SMALL ROUND LOG THAT CROSSES THE TRAIL

SPECIAL HINT: *Roots are as slippery as rocks when wet! Be careful!* These tree roots are searching everywhere for food and water to keep the tree alive. The ground is very rocky in the Smoky Mountains and the roots are doing all they can to feed the tree!!!

_____**10 points**

#7 FIND THE TREE WRAPPED AROUND A BOULDER!!!

20 STEPS PAST THE HUGE HEMLOCK TREE ON THE LEFT OF THE TRAIL—IN A WIDE OPEN AREA BY THE CREEK.

SPECIAL HINT: The tree wrapped around the boulder is on the right of the trail and you'll see what looks like a small cave-like opening under the rock. This yellow birch tree grew right around the rock. Very interesting! There are lots of fascinating natural sights like this in the forests of the Smokies!

_____**10 points**

#8 FIND A SIGN OF A BLACK BEAR!!!

ANYWHERE ALONG THE TRAIL—GO ON TO #9 WHILE
YOU ARE SEARCHING

SPECIAL HINT: This trail is known for a lot of bear activity! Bear drop-pings (scat) are often a shiny blue-black in color in the berry eating season. Another sign of bears is claw marks on trees or torn apart logs where the bear searched for in-sects to eat. Also look for bear prints in muddy areas. Find *any* sign of a bear along this trail to earn the points! By the way, there are about 2,000 black bears in the na-tional park. That means that there are about two bears for every square mile. Now, *how* long is this trail??? All black bears in the Smokies are actually black! Black bears in other parts of our country range in color from off-white to cinnamon to chocolate brown and finally to black!!!

_____**10 points**

#9 FIND THE WALL OF ROOTS!!!

RIGHT SIDE OF THE TRAIL

SPECIAL HINT: A tree was blown over and created a huge "wall of roots." The forest is changing constantly. Wind, rain, snow, hail, lightning, landslides, floods, insects, and temperature changes all affect the environment. This tree faced a very heavy wind and lost the battle. It will now serve a new purpose as a home for many animals and plants!

_____**10 points**

#10 FIND THE TWO YELLOW BIRCH TREES!!! 30 STEPS PAST
THE WALL OF ROOTS—SEARCH ON THE RIGHT FOR TWO BIRCH TREES
STANDING SIDE BY SIDE

SPECIAL HINT: The bark is yellowish or silvery-white in color. The yel-low birch tree bark is shaggy in spots and looks like shreds of paper. The bark has horizontal lines, not vertical like most trees. This tree was very important to Indians and pioneers because its bark has oil in it and burns even when it is wet. Since birch wood burns slowly and gives off lots of heat, mountain folks would use it for baking bread and pies.

_____**10 points**

#11 FIND THE WHITE QUARTZ ROCKS!!! (BREATHE DEEP, IT WILL TAKE A WHILE TO GET THERE) LOOK FOR THE LEANING TREE THAT IS <u>SMACK-DAB IN THE MIDDLE</u> OF THE TRAIL—LOOK UP THE HILL ON THE LEFT TO FIND THE ROCKS

SPECIAL HINT: Quartz is the most common of all minerals and is found throughout the Smokies. There is another really cool quirk of nature at this stop. Turn around and find the rock that is lodged in a tree *at eye level* on the opposite side of the trail! Nature is amazing!!!

_____10 points

#12 FIND THE NURSING TREE TRUNK!!! COUNT BACK 45 STEPS FROM THE LEANING TREE AND QUARTZ ROCKS (#11) TOWARD <u>THE START</u> OF THE TRAIL—LOOK UP THE HILL TO THE RIGHT—AS YOU FACE THE TRAILHEAD

SPECIAL HINT: Find the huge rhododendron shrub that is growing right out of the top of a tall dead tree trunk. The tree trunk is like a "mother" nursing the plant with food and nutrients. This occurs because there is so much rain and moisture in these woods. At this elevation over 80 inches (almost 7 feet) of rain falls each year. You'll see many plants and bushes growing out of stumps and even out of dead trees high off the ground.

_____10 points

#13 FIND THE SLATE HIGHWAY!!! JUST BEFORE YOU REACH THE LOG FOOTBRIDGE

SPECIAL HINT: This rock pathway can be slippery when wet. It is made of slate and Anakeesta rock. Why do we call it a *high*way? It's a *way* to get to *higher* places along this trail! Up ahead . . . Alum Cave Bluffs!!! Mount LeConte!!!

_____10 points

#14 FIND THE YELLOW BIRCH HANDRAIL!!! AT THE NEXT
LOG FOOTBRIDGE

SPECIAL HINT: Think . . . shaggy paper-like bark, yellowish tint, shiny, horizontal lines, used for baking pies . . . ringing any bells?

_____**10 points**

#15 CONDUCT A SCIENTIFIC EXPERIMENT!!! 20 STEPS PAST
THE LOG FOOTBRIDGE

SPECIAL HINT: Find the half-dozen or so evergreen trees on the left side of the trail. Touch the end of a tree needle and if it hurts you have identified a red spruce tree! If it feels soft and you didn't say "Ouch," it is a hemlock! O.K. You're now a forestry scientist . . . Not!!! To be extra sure it is a hemlock, check for two white stripes on the back of each needle.

_____**10 points**

#16 FIND THE JUMBLED UP TREES, ROCKS, STUMPS, AND BUSHES LEFT HERE BY THE 1951 LABOR DAY WEEKEND FLASH FLOOD ON MT. LECONTE!!! AS YOU BEAR TO THE
RIGHT—UP THE HILL

SPECIAL HINT: On Labor Day Weekend in 1951 a powerful storm dumped a huge amount of rain <u>in just 1 hour in one small area on Mt. LeConte!!!</u> The flash flood came hurling down the mountain carrying large trees, boulders, shrubs, rocks, and dirt toward the bottom of the mountain. The debris is still here. Find it and earn the points. Further up the trail is debris from another major storm that occurred in 1993 when a 20-foot avalanche of water crashed down from Mt. LeConte! Do you have your poncho with you???

_____**10 points**

#17 FIND A BLACK-BELLIED SALAMANDER!!! LOOK UNDER ROCKS AND BRANCHES ALONG THE CREEK AND ALONG WET MOSSY BANKS AND IN DAMP AREAS OF THE TRAIL

SPECIAL HINT: There are over 30 different kinds of salamanders in the park. They are camouflaged and very hard to see. Look *very very* closely after you pick up a rock. If you find one, don't put the rock back on top of the salamander because you might hurt it. Go ahead and give yourself the points for any salamander that you see! The black-bellied salamander is over 6 inches long and is probably the largest of the salamanders living on this trail. It has a black belly and often has a double row of light dots on its sides. The hellbender salamander grows to over 2 feet long!!! Whoa!!! The damp area around arch rock is a great place to look.

_____10 points

#18 FIND THE ARCH ROCK AND BENCH!!! YOU CAN'T MISS EITHER OF THESE TREASURES—STRAIGHT AHEAD

SPECIAL HINT: You'll be happy to find both of these treasures! The arch is made of Anakeesta rock which is actually oceanic mud (mud from the ocean) that was squished together *really* . . . I mean <u>really</u> hard. Scientists believe that rock was turned to mud when the continents collided millions of years ago and produced intense pressure and heat. **Anakeesta** is a Cherokee word meaning "Place of the Balsams" referring to the fraser fir trees that grow farther up the mountain. It is hard to believe that where you are walking was once the BOTTOM of an ocean!!! You will now <u>walk right through the center of this rock formation</u>! There are steel cables to help you.

_____10 points

#19 FIND INSPIRATION POINT!!! HIKE QUITE A WHILE—
LOCATED AT THE TOP OF A RIDGE WHERE THE TRAIL TAKES A 90-DEGREE TURN TO THE RIGHT

SPECIAL HINT: The lookout over this rock cliff offers an incredible view of the valleys and hills far below! Are you inspired yet? *Be careful*. You are standing on a rock at over 4,500 feet elevation with a long sheer drop to the bottom! A little red squirrel called the "mountain boomer" is often seen along this trail with the little gray junco bird called the "snowbird." Inspiration Point is on a heath bald, which is an area with lots of low-growth plants like catawba rhododendron, mountain laurel, and sand myrtle *instead* of trees. The catawba rhododendron near Inspiration Point has beautiful purple and pink flowers that bloom in late spring and early summer!

_____**10 points**

#20 FIND THE NEEDLE HOLE IN THE MOUNTAIN!!! STOP
AND LOOK TO YOUR LEFT AS YOU GET TO THE STEEL CABLE HANDRAIL

SPECIAL HINT: Look in the distance and find the round hole that goes ***all the way*** through the top of Little Duck Hawk Ridge! Look along the horizon at the top of the mountains to find the hole. A "duck hawk" is what the mountain folks called the peregrine falcon. The "duck hawk" can dive out of the sky at speeds up to 180 miles per hour as it grabs its prey (other birds) in mid-air!!! Talk about fast food!!! The peregrine falcons were reintroduced to the park in the 1980s and can again be found along this trail.

_____**10 points**

#21 FIND THE ROCK OVERHANG THAT IS ABOUT AS BIG AS A FOOTBALL FIELD!!! ALUM CAVES BLUFF IS SO AWESOME IT WILL TAKE YOUR BREATH AWAY

SPECIAL HINT: Believe me—you— you won't find anything else like the bluffs in these Smoky Mountains! You are standing about 5,000 feet above sea level and are about half-way to Mt. LeConte!!! These cliffs are Anakeesta rock just like the Arch Rock you went through earlier in the hike. The bluffs are not really a cave and there never really was any alum up here! This is a massive rock overhang that was once mined for epsom salts! The sulfur in the bluffs smells a bit like rotten eggs. Be wary of falling icicles in the winter!

_____10 points

CONGRATULATIONS!!!

YOU HAVE JUST COMPLETED A
GREAT SMOKY MOUNTAINS NATIONAL PARK

SCAVENGER HIKE ADVENTURE!!!

<u>Alum Cave Bluffs</u>
<u>Trail to the Bluffs</u>

TEN POINTS FOR EACH ITEM FOUND

TOTAL SCORE _____

CERTIFIED ACHIEVEMENT

LEVEL_____

over 50 to 100 points: <u>**City Slicker**</u>
over 100 to 170 points: <u>**Pioneer Scout**</u>
over 170 points: <u>**Frontier Explorer**</u>

Name(s): _____

_____

Witness(es) thereof: _____

Date: _____

Scavenger Hike Adventure #14

Extremely Extreme Option:
On Up to Mt. LeConte

#22 FIND "GRACIE'S PULPIT"!!! 10–15 MINUTE HIKE PAST THE BLUFFS—SEARCH ON THE LEFT

      SPECIAL HINT: This is a rocky look-out point named after Gracie McNichol, who climbed Mt. LeConte over 200 times, including on her 92nd birthday!!! How old are you?

                                           _____**10 points**

PUT YOUR BOOK AWAY AND ENJOY THE INCREDIBLE 2.5 MILES ON UP TO THE TOP OF MT. LECONTE!!! YOUR NEXT SEARCH ITEM IS 2.5 MILES FROM WHERE YOU ARE STANDING RIGHT NOW!

#23 FIND THE NAME OF THE MAN WHO CARRIED HIS MOTHER TO MT. LECONTE WHILE SHE WAS STRAPPED TO HIS BACK SITTING IN A KITCHEN CHAIR!!! SEARCH IN THE "OFFICE"

      SPECIAL HINT: This is no joke!!! Find the photograph on the wall.

                                           _____**10 points**

#24 FIND THE SNAGS!!!
ON THE MOUNTAIN SLOPES

  SPECIAL HINT: Fraser fir trees and red spruce trees grow up high here on Mt. LeConte. The thousands of dead fraser fir trees (called "snags") surrounding you were infested by the tiny balsam wooly adelgid (a-dell-jid) insect that came from Europe. It killed 95% of the mature trees in the park. You can see how very beautiful these fraser fir trees were because you can find some of the younger generation of trees up on this mountain. Forest rangers hope that some of the young seedlings from a few mature trees that survived the attack up here on Mt. LeConte have inherited a resistance to the bug. They are hopeful that this new generation of trees will re-forest this area of the park.

           _____**10 points**

#25 FIND THE STREET SIGN THAT SAYS LLAMA LANE!!!
BEHIND THE KITCHEN

  SPECIAL HINT: Llamas bring food and clean sheets and pillowcases up to the lodge at Mount LeConte. They trek up on Trillium Gap Trail, one of the five trails that reach this summit. Llamas have smaller hooves than horses and they cause less damage to the trails.

           _____**10 points**

#26 FIND CLIFF TOP!!! AS UNBELIEVABLE AS IT MAY SOUND—
<u>HIKE UP!</u> FOLLOW THE SIGN TO CLIFF TOP!

  SPECIAL HINT: Cliff Top or bust!!! It is only 2/10 of a mile from the rustic cabins and lodges of Mount LeConte. The view is absolutely magnificent on a clear day!!! There is a huge flat rock area at Cliff Top that is suitable for taking an extremely well-deserved break. Enjoy your journey back down. Remember, the journey *is* the destination!

           _____**10 points**

CONGRATULATIONS!!!

YOU HAVE JUST COMPLETED A
GREAT SMOKY MOUNTAINS NATIONAL PARK

SCAVENGER HIKE ADVENTURE!!!

<u>Alum Cave Bluffs Trail to the Bluffs</u>
<u>and</u>
<u>Extremely Extreme Option</u>
<u>On Up to Mt. LeConte</u>

TEN POINTS FOR EACH ITEM FOUND

TOTAL SCORE _____

CERTIFIED ACHIEVEMENT

LEVEL_____

over 50 to 100 points: <u>City Slicker</u>
over 100 to 210 points: <u>Pioneer Scout</u>
over 210 points: <u>Frontier Explorer</u>

Name(s): _____

_____

Witness(es) thereof: _____

Date: _____

MOUNTAIN JOURNAL

MOUNTAIN JOURNAL

MOUNTAIN JOURNAL

MOUNTAIN JOURNAL

MOUNTAIN JOURNAL

MOUNTAIN JOURNAL

MOUNTAIN JOURNAL

Mountain Journal

MOUNTAIN JOURNAL

MOUNTAIN JOURNAL

MOUNTAIN JOURNAL

MOUNTAIN JOURNAL

MOUNTAIN JOURNAL

MOUNTAIN JOURNAL

Keep Exploring the Smokies!
Here Are Some Great Books!!!

We listened to a lot of park rangers, mountain folks, park resident descendants, and other locals to research the hidden treasures. We also studied some great books listed below. Most of them are available in the Great Smoky Mountains National Park visitor centers or at the Great Smoky Mountains Association's on-line bookstore at www.SmokiesStore.org

Alsop, Fred J. III, Birds of the Smokies, Great Smoky Mountains Association, 2001

Boyd, Brian A., Great Smoky Mountains Pocket Companion, Fern Creek Press, 2001

Brewer, Carson, Day Hikes of the Smokies, Great Smoky Mountains Association, 2002

Brewer, Carson, Hiking in the Great Smokies, Newman/National, 1962

Brown, Gary, Outwitting Bears, Living in Bear Country, Lyons Press, 2001

Delaughter, Jerry, Mountain Roads & Quiet Places, Great Smoky Mountains Association, 1986

Duncan, Barbara R., and Brett H. Riggs, Cherokee Heritage Trails Guidebook, In association with the Museum of the Cherokee Indian and University of North Carolina Press, 2003

Dunn Durwood, Cades Cove, The Life and Death of a Southern Appalachian Community, 1818-1837, University of Tennessee Press, 1988

Frome, Michael, Strangers in High Places, The Story of the Great Smoky Mountains, University of Tennessee Press, 1997

Gilmore, Robert, Great Walks, The Great Smokies, Great Walks, Inc., 1992

Great Smoky Mountains Association, Hiking Trails of the Smokies

Grooms, Don, and Oocumma, John, How to Talk Trash in Cherokee, Downhome Publishing, 1989

Hollowell, Anne C., and Barbara G., Fern Finder, Nature Study Guild

Houk, Rose, Great Smoky Mountains National Park, A Natural History Guide, Houghton Mifflin, 1993

Hubbs, Hal; Maynard, Charles; and Morris, David, <u>Time Well Spent, Family Hiking in the Smokies</u>, Third edition, Panther Press, 1995

Jenkins, Ken (photographer), and Brewer, Carson, <u>Great Smoky Mountains National Park</u>, Graphic Arts Center Publishing

Malloy, Johnny, <u>Day and Overnight Hikes in the Great Smoky Mountains National Park</u>, Second Edition, Menasha Ridge Press, 2001

Mooney, James, <u>History, Myths and Sacred Formulas of the Cherokees</u>, originally published by the Bureau of American Ethnology, 1891, Bright Mountain Books, 1992

Ogle, Lucinda Oakley, <u>Remembrances of My Past 93 Years Growing Up in the Smoky Mountains</u>, published by L.O. Oakley, 2002

Oakley, Harvey and Melba, <u>Smoky Mountains Memories and Meditations</u>, Oakley Books, 2003

Oakley, Wiley, <u>Roamin' & Restin'</u>, Oakley Books, 1940

Roop, Peter and Connie, <u>If You Lived With the Cherokee</u>, Scholastic, Inc., 1998

Russell, Gladys and Trentham, <u>Smoky Mountain Family Album</u>, published by G T Russell

Russell, Gladys and Trentham, <u>It Happened in the Smokies</u>, published by author, 1988

Schneider, Bill and Russ, <u>Backpacking Tips</u>, Falcon Publishing, 1998

Shields, Randolph A., <u>The Cades Cove Story</u>, Great Smoky Mountains Association, 1981

Tilley, Stephen G., and Huheey, James E., <u>Reptiles and Amphibians of the Great Smoky Mountains</u>, Great Smoky Mountains Association, 2001

Weals, Vic, <u>Legends of Cades Cove and the Smokies Beyond</u>, Olden Press, 2002

Wise, Kenneth, and Petersen, Ron, <u>A Natural History of Mount LeConte</u>, University of Tennessee Press, 1998

White, Peter (lead author), <u>Wildflowers of the Smokies</u>, Great Smoky Mountains Association, 1996

Wise, Kenneth, <u>Hiking Trails of the Great Smoky Mountains</u>, University of Tennessee Press, 1996

Wuerthner, George, <u>Great Smoky Mountains, A Visitors Companion</u>, Stackpole Books, 2003

ORDER FORM

For entertaining and inspirational speaking engagements or Smoky Mountains hiking seminars for your tour group, hiking club, school group, church group, or business meeting, contact:

LeConte Press
P.O. Box 222
Gatlinburg, TN 37738
865-368-8903, scavengerhike@aol.com

Make check or money order payable to LeConte Press.

Please send _____ books @ $10.95 per book. Postage/shipping costs are $2 for the first book and $1 for each additional book.

On orders sent to a Tennessee address, please add 9.5% per book for sales tax ($12.00 each).

Total amount of your order: $_____

Name:_____ Phone: (_____)_____-_____

Address:_____

City:_____ State:_____ Zip:_____

Paid by check or
Money Order ❏   Visa ❏   MasterCard ❏

Card #_____ Exp. Date_____

Name on Card:_____ Signature:_____